D0097176

THE ONLY WAY OUT
IS THROUGH

THE ONLY WAY OUT
IS THROUGH

MARTE TILTON

THE ONLY WAY OUT IS THROUGH by Marte Tilton
Published by Creation House
A part of Strang Communications Company
600 Rinehart Road
Lake Mary, Florida 32746
www.creationhouse.com

This book or parts thereof may not be reproduced in any form, stored in a retrieval system or transmitted in any form by any means—electronic, mechanical, photocopy, recording or other-wise—without prior written permission of the publisher, except as provided by United States of America copyright law.

Unless otherwise noted, all Scripture quotations are from the King James Version of the Bible.

Scripture quotations marked AMP are from the Amplified Bible, Old Testament copyright © 1965, 1987 by the Zondervan Corporation. The Amplified New Testament copyright © 1954, 1958, 1987 by the Lockman Foundation. Used by permission.

Scripture quotations marked NIV are from the Holy Bible, New International Version. Copyright © 1973, 1978, 1984, International Bible Society. Used by permission.

Scripture quotations marked NKJV are from the New King James Version of the Bible. Copyright © 1979, 1980, 1982 by Thomas Nelson, Inc., publishers. Used by permission.

Scripture quotations marked NLT are from The Holy Bible, New Living Translation, copyright © 1996. Used by permission of Tyndale House Publishers, Inc., Wheaton, IL 60189. All rights reserved.

Scripture quotations marked TLB are from The Living Bible. Copyright © 1971. Used by permission of Tyndale House Publishers, Inc., Wheaton, IL 60189. All rights reserved.

Copyright © 2000 by Marte Tilton
All rights reserved

Library of Congress Catalog Card Number: 00-105711
International Standard Book Number: 0-88419-727-1

0 1 2 3 4 5 6 VERSA 8 7 6 5 4 3 2 1
Printed in the United States of America

To my children,
Amy and Bill, Jon, Marc and Matt,
and to my grandchildren,
Reagan Will and Makena Ann

CONTENTS

CHAPTER 1

THERE IS A
WAY OUT

B ARING MYSELF TO THE WORLD—TO PEOPLE WHO WILL JUDGE WHAT I HAVE done, see the decisions I have made and the way I have lived—makes me feel vulnerable. My story is simply my story, and I do not presume to tell anyone else's. When I have done wrong, I have repented, tried to correct it and move on. My intention here is not to justify, excuse, condemn or judge any part of my story—or anyone whose life has touched mine. But it is my hope that I can help you find a way out of the danger or trouble you may be facing.

Many do not know my story—some only think they know it. My husband, Bob Tilton, was caught in the cross hairs of a *PrimeTime Live* story by Diane Sawyer in 1991. If you saw the story, you probably have no doubt that he is a charlatan and a crook. If you lived the reality as I did, you know how utterly untrue the attacks were. My purpose is to testify to the goodness and sustaining grace of God who kept me and protected my children and me through the destruction of our reputation, the devastation of my divorce and the constant wearing of lawsuits, lawyers and depositions. The Word declares, "The

1

righteous cry out, and the Lord hears, and delivers them out of all their troubles" (Ps. 34:17, NKJV). This is my testimony.

I believe you may recognize the stormy seas I have traveled. You may see yourself floating in the same boat I was in. I believe many people today—even many leaders—are perilously close to capsizing or crashing against some hidden rocks. So I risk, and I write, because I have found some life preservers that may help you and some important principles I can share with you.

Although a portion of my life has been chronicled in the news media, the underlying traps into which I fell have not been revealed. Even though my story once made headlines, the snares I have discovered are no different than those you will experience. I pray that the lessons I have learned will help you to avoid some painful pitfalls, to be strengthened in the Lord, to learn more of who you are in Christ—and maybe even to slay some giants so you can move into your personal promised land.

> "For I know the plans I have for you," declares the Lord,
> "plans to prosper you and not to harm you, plans to give
> you hope and a future."
>
> —Jeremiah 29:11, NIV

God has promised that He will bring us into the place He has for us. Light is shining at the end of *every* tunnel, and the way out is *always* "through."

Where's the Exit?

When we are faced with danger, adversity, troubles or despair, the most common thing we seek is a quick exit to return to our comfort zone or safety. But rarely are quick exits provided in this life, because it is the testing of our faith that makes us strong.

A friend of mine was watching a stage play at the historic Majestic Theater in Dallas recently when he suddenly felt ill.

Glancing around from his balcony seat, he saw the long aisle down which he had come and decided it was too disruptive to leave that way. Instead, he stepped over a few seats to the side, where a green "EXIT" sign shone. As he reached for the door, he noticed it said "Emergency Exit," but he quietly slipped through it anyway. As soon as he crossed the threshold, he knew he had made a mistake. The cold night air immediately revived him, but now he had to reckon with the fact that he was standing on the fire escape—and the door behind him was locked!

Like my friend, when we take the quick way out of a situation, we may actually end up in a deeper mess. The tools for persevering and pushing through to victory are available to all of us—faith, courage, will power, friends, wisdom, prayer and even laughter. Yet in the worst of situations, we tend to feel stripped of power and helpless against the forces arrayed against us. That's when we are tempted with the "easy" way out, which often only sucks us lower until we are consumed in the murky darkness of despair.

No two stories are alike. I have learned that when people remark, "I know exactly how you feel," they really do not. Each of us has been created uniquely. Our personalities, history, knowledge, talent and skills blend with the trouble around us in a way that creates a unique experience, one entirely our own. Those most certain about the meaning and purpose of trouble are generally those who have experienced trouble the least.

My story is different from that of many people because my personal tragedies were played out in newspapers and on television programs for everyone to see. But all humans share the same basic emotions, and the choices I had to make in my circumstances are no different from the choices everyone else has to make in theirs.

What is in our hearts is the greatest factor in whether we sink or swim, continue to fail or pick up and move on. For years I looked for the "promised land" God had for me. I did not understand that my "land" is actually mapped out by God *in my own heart*. That which I plant in my heart from God's Word will grow, bear fruit and multiply. But the tares and weeds of this world that I do not root up will also grow up and multiply.

The first thing to plant in our hearts is the solid knowledge that God loves us, cares for us and will always bring us through. No ditch is too deep, no slander has spread too far, no odds loom too high against us and no consequence for sin is too overwhelming to diminish God's love or to stop Him from bringing us through.

I know the mistakes I have made—clothed in "good works," thinking I was doing the honorable thing, holding everything together and "putting on a front" when all the while the cracks in the foundation were destroying my family, not from without, but from within. I hope you will learn from my mistakes and never fall into the pit. Guard your heart with all diligence, as the writer of Proverbs says in Proverbs 4:23. Follow the commands of our Lord, and you will live a long life in peace with your children after you. (See Proverbs 3:1–2.)

I have no intention of this book being a "kiss and tell" account of my life. That is not my desire, nor would that be beneficial to you. The details that I disclose in this book are given only so you can understand what I went through and how our precious Lord met me at my point of deepest need. I know He will meet you, too.

I want to tell you how I got through the destruction of my life. The things I tell you about my life will be told for one purpose only—to let you know that I know what it's like to have unendurable things hit you...one after another...after another... and to have to manage them all at once seemingly by yourself. I did not have the resources within myself to cope with my circumstances—and neither do you. But I learned how to find my needs met in Christ and in the goodness of His strength and blessings. I want to help you in the process of

4

discovering that the only way out is through—*and you can go through.*

Regardless of where you find yourself today—no matter how hot your battle, how cool your spirit, how high your barriers or how low your despair—the only way out of your difficulties is through faith in Jesus Christ.

CHAPTER 2

BEGINNINGS
AND BLESSINGS

M Y STORY BEGAN SIMPLY. DURING THE SIXTIES WHEN AMERICA'S young people challenged their parents' values, I joined in, wondering if the values I had learned in my little East Texas hometown were true—especially if God were real.

When I was in my early twenties, I married. My husband, Bob, and I were a good match, even though we were opposites. We had perhaps married for all the wrong reasons, but it turned out so right after we were Christians. When we first met, I was in charge of a "one-girl" office in Dallas that placed engineers. He was a nice guy who came in for work, then called me later to invite me out. We dated off and on for a year, then decided one day to marry. Even though it was popular to shock parents and live together at the time, we decided our parents were too conservative for that. Perhaps we were too and just did not know it. We married before a judge, the only one I thought I would ever appear before in my life.

Our strengths matched each other's weaknesses. I was structured; he was spontaneous. I was the detail; he was the broad stroke. I was practical; he was a dreamer. I was realistic; he was emotional. We both had our weaknesses. Everyone does.

When my husband and I married, neither of us were Christians—or anything close to it. For a number of years we lived a rather wild life, although my husband seemed to try to pull me further into some activities—like experimenting with drugs—than I wanted to go. My personality is such that I like to be in control of myself, and so for me, drugs were not a good thing. In addition, I would not be happy in that lifestyle of laziness and blown minds with no productivity in life.

About the time our first child was on the way, inexplicable and eerie things started occurring in our home, which I am sure were demonic in origin. For example, sometimes as I worked to prepare our first child's nursery, the room would become ice cold. Our dog refused to go in that room. A self-proclaimed "exorcist" came over once and locked himself in that room. When he came out, he told us not to worry because "the spirits are not here to hurt you." That scared me even more! Feeling alone and afraid, I cried out, "God, if You are real, will You please help me?"

One evening I flipped on the television and saw America's evangelist, Billy Graham, leading an altar call. The song "Just As I Am" was playing in the background. All alone, I knelt in my living room and said, "God, if You're real, I want to commit my life to You, but You have to help me."

A few weeks later, three young men and a woman called Granny Rose knocked on our door. They had brought a guitar, and they sang some songs for my husband and me. They read some passages of Scripture, and then went in that room and took authority over any demonic presence. That night my husband and I both followed them in praying the "sinner's prayer" and committed our lives to Christ. Immediately our house became normal, even the creepy room.

My husband's response to his newfound faith was to

announce that he wanted to purchase a tent and trailer and to travel and teach people about Jesus. His zeal was genuine and frightening to me, a shy, conservative country girl. Yet God seemed to restrain him, and we settled down to raise a family.

A few years later, he convinced me to leave the security of my administrative job and stay home with our children, ages one and three at the time. This was a big thing for me. We had always been blessed of the Lord when both of us were working. We had talked about our dreams for our family, and I felt there were things that I could do better for the family if I was working. But I made the decision to do as my husband asked.

Just a few short months later, he called me from where he was working on a construction project. "Listen to this verse of Scripture," he said excitedly. Then he read these words: "Say not ye, There are yet four months, and then cometh harvest? Behold, I say unto you, Lift up your eyes, and look on the fields; for they are white already to harvest" (John 4:35). "Now is the time," he told me. "It's time for me to go into the ministry. I have put the house up for sale. I'm buying a travel trailer and a tent, and I'm going into the ministry."

I was panic-stricken. "God, please do not allow our home to sell," I prayed. We had just purchased a modest house. Yet it sold within days. Hurt and angry, I poured out my frustrations to God. Like a gentle, loving Father, God reassured me with the following scripture:

> There is no man that hath left house, or brethren, or sisters, or father, or mother, or wife, or children, or lands, for my sake, and the gospel's, but he shall receive an hundredfold now in this time, houses, and brethren, and sisters, and mothers, and children, and lands, with persecutions; and in the world to come eternal life.
>
> —MARK 10:29–30

This was a monumental moment in my life. Even though I had not been a Christian as I was growing up, I had always had a sensitivity toward God. As a child I occasionally attended Sunday school in a Baptist church, but I had no knowledge of a personal relationship with God. I always wanted to know God. I always wanted to serve God, but I did not know how. Sometimes as a young child I would be playing out in the yard and would stop because I seemed to recognize the presence of God there with me. I'd look up toward heaven and say, "Are You here, God? Are You here?"

But the one thing I knew I never wanted to be was a minister's wife! Yet all at once that was exactly what my husband was asking me to be.

We sold everything and bought a truck, a tent, a trailer and a Toyota. I drove the car while my husband drove the truck pulling the trailer. Our first stop was Lakewood Church in Houston.

We had never met him before, but Pastor John Osteen called me out of the huge congregation during the first service we attended and said, "God wants to say something to you. Come to the front." Trembling with embarrassment, I walked to the front where Pastor Osteen said, "You have had turmoil about giving up all, but God has won the battle by you giving up your security and going into the ministry. Many will come to you for counsel. Your food barrels will never run dry. You will have riches and gold, but Jesus will be your security. As God gave Noah the sign of the rainbow, God also gives it to you today— He will never leave you nor forsake you."

That prophetic word from a man of God whom I had never met before had a lasting impact on my life. Suddenly I recognized that not only was my husband asking me to follow him into a life of ministry—God was validating that decision. He was going with me. He was promising that He would be my security, my sustenance and my companion on the journey.

Shortly after that service, as I read my Bible, I received an incredible promise. God spoke to my heart and said, "Now you are My ambassador."

At that time, this did not mean much to a young woman from an east Texas steel mill town. Some years later, though, in the midst of building a church He spoke to me again, "Now you are My ambassador."

When we began our "traveling evangelist" ministry, I insisted I did not want to bring up my children "on the road" with a slip-shod existence. My husband agreed with me. We were a team—friends and partners in agreement to conduct our Father's business with integrity. We talked together, worked together and dreamed together.

For a year, my husband and I ministered in the tent, pulling our house behind that big truck, from town to town. We sold greeting cards to help with the expenses. At the end of one year, we parked the trailer in Houston and began building fences to make ends meet. We received good money, but it was hard work—hot in the summer and cold in the winter.

My older children still remember those lean days. Although the children were very small, they coped well. We had a little bicycle and a tricycle for them. They played in a cardboard box and slept on the sofa bed at night.

I can remember one day in February when we were building a new fence at a subdivision in Houston. The kids were all bundled up, but they were still freezing. As my husband and I worked, Amy and Jon wandered over to the back window of a nearby house, put their hands up to the window and stood there gazing at the fireplace inside. The woman came to the door, invited my children into the warmth and made cookies for them. It was a very humble time for us. "There has to be a better purpose in our life than this," I cried out to God. I praised God for being able to make the money that we were making, but I knew that He had something different for us—something greater.

We were relieved when we were called to Irving, Texas, to

interview for a church pastorate in 1976. Immediately, we knew that wasn't the church for us, but it started us praying in a new direction instead of pursuing the traveling evangelistic route. We agreed together that God was calling us to pioneer a "family church," and my husband felt God tell him it was to be in Farmers Branch, Texas.

Driving through the suburb of Dallas, we found an available YMCA building and started our church with the four in our family plus Jimmy and Joann Collis and Phyllis Dias. We had to go in there every week and clean it with Lysol because it smelled like tennis shoes. But I was certainly happy to settle down in a home with a foundation and long-running hot water. Our first service was held March 7, 1976, with just the seven people mentioned above in attendance.

It was not long before that YMCA building became unavailable. We drove around the parameters of Farmers Branch praying, "Where can we move? Help us, God, we have to move." One day we passed by an old warehouse. It was huge, and we thought, *We could never afford that. We have just a handful of people... maybe fifty or sixty people... so how in the world could we ever afford that?*

Filled with faith, my husband went to the bank to discuss its purchase. It was in foreclosure, and they agreed to lease it to us for a thousand dollars a month. That left no money to remodel the place. So we took our kids down there and hung tile, painted and did what we could to make it into a church. It was the middle of the summer and so hot that even with air conditioning, we used water hoses to spray down the walls for the evening service. We built a section in the back of the warehouse that seated about one hundred fifty people.

Before long we outgrew that little section, so we expanded the seating throughout the entire warehouse. God blessed those humble beginnings, and we saw continual growth.

Word of Faith Family Church was definitely cutting edge. Two years after we started the church in 1976, I had a vision to start a school. We opened the school in the fall of 1978 with over one hundred children. Enrollment eventually swelled to three hundred fifty in twelve grades, with a day-care center as well.

My relationship to Jesus was so precious to me. I could not imagine letting Him down, so I threw myself into learning what it meant to be an ambassador for Him. I met with Sir Lionel Luckhoo, former ambassador from Guyana and Barbados, and studied etiquette, deportment, events planning and culinary arts.

At first, my vision was for children. Later it broadened for the nation. My husband's vision was for the masses. The best way to reach them was through television. He and I were quite a partnership. As a husband-and-wife team, we launched a daily television program called *Daystar*. Because my husband had asked me to assume the duties of general manager for the church, I administrated the daily operations, working all morning in the office. Then I joined my husband on camera, returning to my office to put in more hours before going home. We also started *Sunday Morning Live* in the early eighties, televising our Sunday morning services live nationwide.

Within ten years we had eight thousand members with well over two thousand satellite affiliate churches. We employed over eight hundred people. I even had increase in my children! More than ten years after the first two were born, I gave birth to two more boys, two years apart.

We supported missions endeavors by the dozens. We built hospitals and funded mobile medical clinics, supported schools and orphanages, dug water wells and gave toward every kind of mission project imaginable all over the world.

Driving around in a truck and trailer as itinerant evangelists at the beginning of our ministry, we had a dream of sharing with little communities around the country what they could not receive personally because they could not afford having one of the "big ministries" come in. When we started the church, we held to our dream, and in 1981, when our congregation was large enough to sustain it, we established the first satellite network for churches. Thousands of churches in Canada, Mexico and Central America were able to receive our monthly seminars through their own satellite dishes (which, incidentally, were enormous back then). We were so excited that through us the gospel could reach any little church, enabling every believer to hear the Word of God.

As a result of the satellite ministry's phenomenal success, we ended up with excess income, which we lavished on those satellite pastors. Many of them could never afford a vacation, so we flew them and their spouses to places like Acapulco or Florida for a combination vacation and conference. Workshops equipped them with tools for their churches. We pulled out all stops for those pastors, loving them for their service to the Lord—service we knew was many times unheralded and often unknown.

Then my husband launched the *Success-N-Life* national television program. Through that outreach, we documented at least three thousand conversions to Christ each month. People were saved in our services every Sunday, often by the hundreds. My husband was a great soulwinner. I did not know personally anyone who was a greater soulwinner during those years apart from Billy Graham, through whose ministry I was saved.

Besides the thousands of salvations, we documented dozens of healings each month. Our files were full of testimonies. People were healed physically and financially, and they were delivered from bondages. Not every report was legitimate, so we documented every case thoroughly before reporting it. The front of the church balcony was decorated with medical equipment from healed people who left it behind at church because they no longer needed it. We had so many healings that from time to time we took the paraphernalia down and started the collection all over again.

The healings and salvations were not limited merely to us personally. My husband was a "fisherman" who inspired others to fish. People in the congregation took God at His Word because they saw His power, and they set out to evangelize their neighborhoods and their workplaces. People brought their friends, and their friends were saved. Timid people gave others a tape, and they were saved. Bolder people witnessed personally, drawing hundreds into the kingdom of God.

Since those days, there have been a lot of hurtful things said about Bob and the ministry God gave us. Some of those things have been true—many others have been completely unfounded. But I know for certain that at one time both our hearts were right before God, and the man I was married to was a man of intense devotion to God. Whatever else he thought or did, then or now, I remember him back then as a man of God and a man of prayer.

THE BIRTH OF A SCHOOL

IN 1985 WE CHANGED THE SCHOOL'S NAME TO LEXINGTON ACADEMY, CHANGED the format from the Accelerated Christian Education Program to classroom-style and became accredited. I helped develop the curriculum, which taught students who they were in Christ, their duty to defend their country and how to enter the workplace carrying the banner of the Lord Jesus Christ.

In addition to the regular curriculum, we taught goal-setting, dressing for success, etiquette, protocol and corporate protocol. We even held an annual cotillion ball and took the seniors to tea to hone their social skills. I was very involved in these activities. The students learned how to write résumés and go on interviews. An outstanding history teacher, Glen Lehman, taught the principles of the founding of America. To strengthen the school's "God and country" theme, Mr. Lehman established our own fife and drum corps, made up strictly of the school's honors students. We bought authentic handmade woolen uniforms (patterned after uniforms designed by George Washington), along with leather boots, wigs and drums. The corps' performance in the latter years was like nothing this side of the president's own. The corps performed for both the governor of Texas and the U. S. ambassador to Great Britain and participated in meetings of major corporations and at other events like the Crystal Charity Ball of Dallas. The corps even presented the colors at a Thanksgiving Day Dallas Cowboys' football game at Texas Stadium.

Our regular instrumental bands and vocalists won state competitions under the leadership of our music director, who had an uncanny ability to draw out of students their very best. Our athletic teams won state championships. We won vocal and academic competitions. We were like a model school, with state-of-the-art equipment, a library, gymnasium, band hall and all the "extras"—all provided by the church as a small part of the missions outreach.

The church television equipment was made available to the students as a broadcast journalism elective. In the years following the *PrimeTime Live* debacle, the church could not afford a crew, so the students ran the entire *Sunday Morning Live* program as interns. Many of those students went on to become professional broadcasters.

The young people of that church and school were outstanding! I remember a couple of young men volunteering to mow the church lawns. Then, when we needed volunteers to run television cameras, they offered. They continued to help in any and every way. Today both of these young men are engaged in the television departments of large ministries.

The people were outstanding! We ran two Sunday morning services. This was considered enormous, and we were counted as one of the new megachurches that were springing up. Our members became involved in patriotism, in doing what was right and fighting for just causes. I was invited, along with people such as Pat Robertson, Jerry Falwell and Beverly LaHaye, to presidential briefings at the White House concerning Christian issues in our country, to the Rose Garden and to meet with Elizabeth Dole, who served at that time as President Reagan's special assistant. I remember fighting for the "cause" alongside a young, idealistic congressman with a burning goal to restore our country's freedoms. His name was Newt Gingrich. Those were heady days!

I took groups to Washington, D.C., to learn our way around the halls of Congress and to talk with congressmen and senators about our concerns. Back then some of our chief issues were education in America, humanism being taught in public schools and the establishment of Christian schools. When our legal counsel said the church could no longer be involved in political activities because of our status as a nonprofit corporation, I encouraged the school children to learn patriotism to both God and country.

By the mideighties, the church was becoming so large we rented the Dallas Convention Center on Easter Sundays, which was trendsetting at the time. Our July Fourth productions also brought out crowds by the droves. In 1984 we hosted the National Day of Prayer with a live televised event from Constitution Hall in Washington, D.C.

In addition to all that, the church had all-night prayer services attended by hundreds, and the early-morning prayer meetings were attended by many on their way to work. The staff would pray in the sanctuary for an hour every morning when we got to work. My husband spent hours praying in a prayer room and in his closet, lying on the prayer requests that were sent to us through the mail.

The majority of the prayer requests that we received were sent to us along with a donation of money. We were very careful to ensure that every need was prayed over. The money that came through the mail went to a lock box at the post office, and from there it was then overnighted to the bank along with church offerings. Bank tellers removed the money and a data processing center processed it, overnighting all prayer requests to the church. After my husband prayed over them, they were sent back to the data processing center for ninety-day storage. I oversaw every detail.

For some time we had a policy with the data processing center that instructed them to incinerate the prayer requests after ninety days. At some point the data processing center decided, due to environmental concerns, to recycle the paper instead of incinerating it. I was never informed of this change of policy—an oversight that was soon to cause us great devastation and hurt.

At the time, I was oblivious to anything that could ever hurt us. I was working six days a week and making three meals a day for four children who were each the apple of my eye. I could not imagine a more satisfying life, nor could I have dreamed that I was making some fatal errors.

This period of expanding ministry that was overflowing with the blessings of God drew to an end. We would soon have our worlds turned upside down—both as a family and as a church body.

CHAPTER 3

A DOWNWARD
SPIRAL

A LTHOUGH WE ENJOYED PHENOMENAL GROWTH IN OUR MINISTRY DURING
the early ten-year period, at times there were challenges
that seemed almost insurmountable. At one point, we
suffered a huge financial loss in our satellite television ministry.
Another large loss came when a postal worker who was hooked
on drugs skimmed letters from our box, opened them, threw
away the checks and kept the cash—stealing nearly a million
dollars. That period of time was my first major test in trusting
God—we had to overcome a deficit of more than a million dollars due to these two financial losses. I was shaken by the stag-
gering figures on the bills I could not pay, but God was gracious.
We came through, paying off every bit of debt, including that on
all our properties and equipment. We even built a reserve fund.

But while we were building a solid base of ministry, meeting
challenge after challenge in the day-to-day business of running the ministry, the enemy had launched an insidious attack
against us—one that would eventually shake us to the very
core. John 10:10 alerts us to the tactics of Satan: "The thief
cometh not, but for to steal, and to kill, and to destroy." Over

the next few years we would experience this firsthand. And he did not level his attack at only the external things that he could steal—like ministry, money and possessions. He had come to steal, kill and destroy our very souls! The seeds of compromise and deception had been planted and, as you will read in later chapters, would reap a harvest of despair and grief.

In 1987 my husband became chronically ill with an immune system breakdown, which doctors said he developed from ink and dry-cleaning solvent he absorbed as he lay on prayer requests in the closet. It appeared that the immune system breakdown caused some mild strokes, causing him to lose part of his memory and to become allergic. The doctors said he needed to reduce stress to build his immune system, otherwise he could have a major stroke and die.

I learned how to cook holistic health foods to help him cope with the illness, but the diet regimen I worked so hard to develop for him was not enough to correct his symptoms. In 1988 he decided to take the doctors' recommendation to move to a better climate where he would have less stress, and we packed up our baby, toddler and two teens and moved to California.

It was a difficult move for me. I had to uproot the children from the school they had attended for years and place them in new schools. By this time we had a huge staff, an annual budget of roughly seventy million dollars and a large television ministry. As the church's general manager, I managed the ministry by long distance, flying in monthly to meet with the managers. About the only emotion I allowed myself to feel during this time was pure exhaustion. On the other hand, my husband's health seemed to improve with the move to California. He flew to Dallas twice monthly to preach on Sunday mornings and spent a great deal of time away from home speaking at international crusades. The pastoral staff handled the other ministry details on a day-to-day basis for him. I don't know when I noticed a tone of disrespect in my husband's voice, but I know our marriage began to suffer from the long absences and long work hours.

When my two oldest children returned to Texas to graduate from high school and attend college in 1990, I became fed up with rattling around in a huge house in California with just my two youngest, and we soon moved back to Texas.

While we had been in California, a Dallas "homeless" minister, who has since publicly announced that a major network paid him for his services, began reporting alleged misdeeds of our church. Upon our return, local rumors turned into news stories that reached the national press. Then came the one-hour televised *PrimeTime Live* newsmagazine in 1991 that "exposed" us and two other ministers.

That night we sat in our new home in Dallas with friends to watch the report. It depicted us as uncaring frauds, basing much of their information on the alleged misdeeds reported by the minister who had attacked us publicly. We were accused of not praying over the hundreds of prayer requests that were sent to us and of having unlimited, proprietary access to the funds sent to the church as donations. At one point, they showed mountains of prayer requests that I had believed had been incinerated. Even though I had created what I thought were airtight procedures to ensure integrity, the data processing firm had opted to recycle the requests for environmental reasons.

The local network affiliate followed up the national report with a prepared news story on us, interviewing someone from the attorney general's office who assured viewers that an investigation was underway, giving the public the impression that the allegations were true. That was the first time we had heard of any government action. That our government would believe such lies stunned me. I was shocked to discover that a person like this self-proclaimed "televangelist watchdog" could give "evidence" I knew to be untrue to the media, who in turn could make up a story to declare us guilty. I was also shocked that the

American people and government agencies would instantly believe it was fact.

We had expected that there would be a story because of calls from ABC. ABC's Diane Sawyer had even come to a Sunday service to attempt to get an interview with Bob.

We all sat motionless and speechless during the entire program. Overnight, we became objects of public ridicule and a flurry of legal action. From then to the present, I was personally named in over a dozen lawsuits ranging from personal suits to legal fraud to insurance suits.

The morning after the broadcast, an FBI agent and a postal inspector walked into our bank to demand all the church records. As promised on television the night before, we immediately received notice from the attorney general's office that they intended to place the church into receivership and appoint a trustee. That office also pressed to acquire every church member's personal records. On this point we fought all the way to the United States Supreme Court—where we prevailed. It was grossly wrong to demand private records of church members.

We faced numerous lawsuits from ministry donors. These lawsuits ranged from accusations of non-response to requests for prayer to fraud and intentional infliction of pain for sending mail to deceased partners on the list. My husband pressed a personal lawsuit against the network and all involved in the television program. The Internal Revenue Service (IRS) soon joined the fracas, conducting a massive audit that lasted three intense years.

Because I managed the church's finances and was considered a copastor, I was individually named in every lawsuit along with my husband. I worked feverishly for months on all the documentation the lawyers needed to fight our legal battles. At the same time, I had IRS auditors in and out of my office and calling weekly. I worked diligently to dig for information with which to defend us, and I faced continual depositions and witness stands over the next seven years. Pieces of the mess still remain today.

God had spoken to me in California before we moved back to Dallas in 1990, saying, "You are seeing the beginning of the end." At that time I did not understand what He meant, but I often thought of it in the coming years. I kept trying to make everything work out, but nothing I did was ever going to change the course we were on. A shift had taken place in our hearts.

A Lost Church

Early in 1992 we had a hearing at the state capitol in Austin regarding the attorney general's attempt to put the church into receivership. They basically wanted to say that a secular person would have to take charge. I was very nervous at that hearing. It was the first time I had been in front of a judge since the day I was married. But I held my ground. The attorney general's lawyers were testy with me, so I was testy back. "Is that what you mean?" they asked me several times.

"No, that isn't what I mean; this is what I mean..." I responded to their questions each time.

Finally my lawyer objected to the harassment of the attorney general's lawyers. The federal judge looked over his glasses at them and said, "I think this witness can take care of herself!" That was my first education in testifying, and I had no idea that line of questioning could go on for hours, days, weeks and even years in lawsuits.

In the battle with the attorney general, we won in the federal courts. But the judge determined that since the church was a corporation, the attorney general still had a gateway to continue his investigation. The threat of receivership and a secular trustee had caused me to fear that office even more than I feared the IRS, and I only feared the IRS because I had been taught to. The IRS turned out to be friendly! They were a cake walk compared to the rest.

The church's attorney called me after the judge's decision in

March 1992 and said we needed to make a quick decision. He said the attorney general's office was coming after us, but if we dissolved the corporation and simply became a "church," we could save the church for the congregation.

A nagging voice arose from my heart. The lawyer's rationale puzzled me. I had always been told that we needed to be incorporated to give tax-exempt receipts for charitable donations. I pressed the attorney as to how we could dissolve the corporation, and he assured me it had already been done by the Catholic church. In our case, I was told, "Your husband will simply become the 'pope.'"

"He's in no condition to be the 'pope' of anything!" I said. Bob often said he was "on the edge" at that time, insinuating that he was suicidal. Besides, he was never at church...never in the office...always out of town in Florida. He was not there for the congregation. I asked what position I would have in such a scheme since I was a founder and vice president of the current corporation. He said I would be part of a "college of elders," which could easily be appointed *after* we completed the paperwork.

I discussed the plan by telephone with the only other board member for the church. We were both against the new structure, but felt that since our legal advisors were in a position to know more than we knew, we should do it to protect the church and the members of our congregation from losing what they had built. The church's lawyers knew the "magic words" for me to hear were, "It's best for the church and the congregation."

Anything seemed better than the attorney general's office naming a secular trustee to oversee the church. The board member and I puzzled over how we could protect our church members without giving control to my husband, whose behavior seemed erratic at best. We finally told the lawyer we would only agree to dissolve the incorporated church, but neither of us agreed with the proposed structure. We said we wanted to hear more about it and that it would need to be further defined. We thought he agreed to that.

Ever so quickly papers were drawn up to dissolve the corporation and transfer all the assets to Word of Faith Church. In March of 1992, we met in my husband's office and signed the papers. Little did we know that even as we signed the papers to dissolve the corporation, a five-page document had already been prepared for the new "church." This document only needed to be signed by my husband. When the matter was discussed with the congregation, members were simply told that a "college of elders" would be established. It never was. Suddenly, not one person in that marvelous congregation could say one thing about church business, including me.

It wasn't until the time of my divorce in the early months of 1993 that all the filthy ramifications of what had happened in my husband's office that day came to light. Signing those papers had been the greatest mistake of my life. With the stroke of a pen, we had lost the church. It still mortifies me to realize I was tricked by my husband and our church's lawyer. As a result, the church congregation, with those faithful members who had stuck it out with us through months of chaos, eventually disintegrated without receiving so much as a word of thanks for all their faithful support.

When my husband divorced me, many of the lawsuits were still pending and had not been resolved. Although I was removed from my job and physically barred from entering the church buildings, I was greatly interested in protecting those who had been a part of our former ministry. On court days, I would show up at court alone and leave alone. The lawyers did not give me the time of day. Yet God honored the fight, and no one went to jail. I believe God did that—not the lawyers.

THE UNKNOTTING OF A MARRIAGE

DURING THE LATE EIGHTIES WHEN WE WERE LIVING AT OUR CALIFORNIA HOME, I became terribly distraught and deeply wounded. I was far from home and friends, with two teens, two toddlers, an eight-hundred-employee staff miles away and an enormous church budget on my shoulders. My husband traveled almost all of the time, and when he was home he spent his time with his friends. He often became testy and irritable or noncommunicative with me.

Shortly before we returned to Texas, he exploded with anger because I would not agree to buy a television station. He could have bought it without me—indeed, that is exactly what he did a couple of years later when we were right in the middle of all the lawsuits that followed the *PrimeTime Live* telecast—but instead, he announced he was going to divorce me over it. I was completely caught by surprise. This was the first overt sign that he was truly unhappy. Although my husband relented and did not pursue a divorce, that storm continued, putting me on a roller coaster of emotions for several years to come.

One hot October morning in 1992, shortly after my daughter had become engaged, my husband and I had an argument about his dream to develop a multilevel corporation. Corporations fall under the jurisdiction of the state attorney general, and we were in hot water with ours already because the church was incorporated. I did not want another corporation for the attorney general to engage in court. I had been called to identify evidence in a deposition that day, and he was angry that I was going. I didn't think I had a choice.

The deposition was so stressful, compounded by our early-morning argument, that my blood pressure rose, and I suddenly felt ill. I drove myself straight to my doctor's office during the lunch recess. As I lay in the chilly examination room, for the first time I felt completely on my own, needing help and having no one to care for me. The doctor refused to discharge me from his office because my blood pressure was at stroke level. With all the stress, I had never seen the signs of high blood pressure—like dizziness—and I did not feel a thing until I was on the verge of having a stroke. But my physical condition was nothing compared to the sobering reality of what my life was becoming. After all the friends and family for all those years, I suddenly felt desperately alone.

I could not find my husband, so I called a friend who finally tracked him down—at the vacation home we had bought in Florida! I have no idea how he got to Florida that fast or why he went. I was too numb even to think.

A couple of weeks after his sudden departure, my husband returned and once again said he wanted a divorce. But when I demanded to know why, he hung his head and cried, saying he wanted to work it out. He even suggested that we would celebrate our twenty-fifth anniversary in a few months in grand style.

In May 1993, we went out for our anniversary with some relatives to a "hole-in-the-wall" Italian restaurant where my husband had reserved a private room. As a gift, he gave me a beautiful ring that I had admired. But all was not well. With others around all the time, it was obvious he did not want to be alone with me.

I was totally confused—one minute he was telling me he loved me; the next he was accusing me of different things and acting jealous of my knowledge.

In mid-June, a month after our daughter's wedding, I agreed to meet my husband for a mini-vacation he wanted to take in conjunction with a crusade where he was speaking. While eating dinner at a restaurant one night, he disappeared, saying he would be right back. But he never came back. Tired of waiting at the table, I finally went back to the hotel room and found a note under a single yellow rose that said simply, "Goodbye." All his clothes and bags were gone. I was terribly distraught, thinking he had gone off to kill himself. I did not know the difference between a suicide note and a "Dear John" letter!

I went back home to Dallas, where I waited for him to

return home. When he finally came back, he gave me no explanation as to why he had left me alone. But he insisted that we follow through with our plans to take a trip to our Florida home with another couple that same month. So, on June 30, 1993, I packed up our two youngest sons and left for what I hoped would be a time of relaxation and reconciliation. I did not know that would be the last day I would ever see my office.

One night in Florida, as we talked late into the night, he stood up and announced he was leaving. He raised his voice to say, "You don't have a job anymore. You are not allowed to enter the church offices ever again, and in fact, don't ever return to Dallas!"

He packed his bags—and he was gone.

I stayed on in Florida. I suppose that deep down I never really believed what he was saying. I was simply in denial. I kept thinking that he would come to his senses as he had before. In a few weeks I decided to return to Dallas.

The church attorney and Bob reduced my salary and told me that my office would be at the school. I began administrating the school's operation only, instead of the church's as well.

When I saw my husband at home, he was in a wonderful mood and spoke excitedly about the divorce—just as if we had launched a new program to save souls. One day he called me at work to say he was with a lawyer and needed the children's social security numbers. I sat there dumbfounded that this was all really happening. I was angry at him, and confused.

THE LIGHTS GO ON

ONE DAY MY HUSBAND AND HIS ATTORNEY CAME TO MY OFFICE. MY HUSBAND'S divorce attorney said he would represent both of us together to come up with an amicable divorce agreement. "That way you won't have to be served," he said. By then, I had been served with so many papers so many times that I no longer feared the process. Besides, being served with divorce papers could in no way compare to the absolute heartbreak of the reality of losing my husband of almost twenty-five years and the father of my four children. Friends helped me make the decision to find my own attorney.

Three days later, the lights went on for me. A deposition meeting regarding one of the lawsuits turned into a five-hour grilling, and much of the questioning turned out to be about my divorce. To my knowledge, the details about the divorce were completely secret between my husband, his lawyer and me. If the opposing attorney knew the details, someone in our camp had tipped him. It felt as if a gate opened and Doberman pinschers pounced on me. For five hours the lawyers badgered me, trying to get me to crack. But I had never hidden anything on the stand. The growing suspicion that my husband led a double life was the only thing I ever hid—from the church, from my children and from myself. Even when I had returned to Dallas from that devastating "vacation" in Florida, I had found a woman preaching in the services and seemingly occupying my husband's time, yet I had never allowed myself to become suspicious. I never dreamed she would one day become my husband's second wife.

When I came home that evening, I sprawled across my bed and stared at the ceiling, completely deflated and exhausted. Sometime during that night as I lay in the darkness, I made the huge discovery that I no longer needed to protect him.

In the morning I told him, "I will not cover for you any longer. And I will not live in this house and act as if we are a happy family. Nor will I cover for your long absences at the office any more. If you are going to get a divorce," I told him, "then go get a divorce."

That is exactly what he did. That morning he told our two youngest sons, one of whom cried, and then he took them out to ride go-carts. "Everything will be OK," he told the boys. "I'll be more of a father to you now than ever. Besides, you know that your mom and I never got along."

The next morning, Sunday, August 15, he came down from the study to tell me he would be announcing the divorce. "Don't go to church today."

But I still didn't really get it.

That morning as my older children and I sat on the front row like always, and the younger two children attended the children's church, he announced we would be divorcing. Almost as a postscript, he added, "If you're a church member who doesn't like this decision, you can leave. If you're an employee, resign."

"Noooo....!" The sound of one church member's cry still rings in my ears; it probably echoes in the minds of almost three thousand people who attended church that morning. Immediately, a stunned hush fell over the congregation, except for the agonized echo of "Noooo...!" It was the heart-wrenching cry we all felt but could not find the voice to give.

After that church service, some church members came to me in tears, saying they could not subject their families to this kind of leadership. Attendance had been slowly dropping since the 1991 *PrimeTime Live* program—and would continue to fall until only a handful remained.

The staff had already been isolated for some time, with my husband being gone so often. They only knew bits and pieces of what was wrong. They kept their questions largely among their closest friends. As the church began to totter and fall, the entire mess became their story as much as it was mine or anyone's. They saw the children's and my photos removed from the office walls and from the sanctuary. They were ordered to edit my name out of all our books.

The congregation knew and understood even less—except that something was desperately wrong. I know my husband had been advised that people would not leave the church if we divorced. But they did.

The congregation had been longsuffering, patient, faithful and loyal. They had made banners, marched for our rights and endured criticism for their church choice. They had defended me, my husband and my family. They had put their time and their reputations on the line, and they were completely shocked and hurt with the way they were repaid. For many, they could no longer tolerate what was happening in their church home. Some left the church to attend other churches. Some left, never to darken a church door again. For those I am so deeply grieved. As I have thought about these individuals while writing this book, I have spent many sleepless nights. I have wondered often if my doing things differently—responding differently—could have helped to provide a far different outcome.

Lethal Legal Games

I RECEIVED A CALL FROM ONE OF THE CHURCH'S LAWYERS WHO ADVISED ME TO LET Charlie, my husband's divorce attorney, handle my divorce so I wouldn't eat up my money in attorney fees. "Texas is a no-fault divorce state," he told me. "If someone says they're divorcing you, you have no choice. You are getting a divorce. And there is no alimony." I hired my own attorney anyway.

Months after my divorce ordeal began, the lawyer I had hired told me honestly that if I pursued a large divorce settlement, our names would once again appear as front-page headlines, probably daily for a period of time. However, he believed he could have the dissolution of the church corporation overturned and also win a settlement against my husband. I had a huge decision to make. I knew that not only had my children suffered shame and humiliation, but everyone in our church family had endured mockery for attending our church. Besides that, the entire body of Christ had been embarrassed by the *PrimeTime Live* telecast, and I did not want to fuel the media fires again. The price tag for coming out "on top" financially was to open the floodgate once again to public ridicule and release more details of our lives on the lurid pages of newspapers.

In my emotional state during those days, with what felt like the weight of the reputation of the body of Christ sitting squarely on my shoulders, I decided the price tag for fighting in the media was too great. I agreed in the divorce for a portion of what we personally owned in our own names. Although I had always put money away in a savings account, my husband had remodeled our Florida beach house the previous year, depleting the account considerably. In the agreement, after I had my portion, my husband would have the rest and would keep control of our only home, as well as of the millions in church assets.

In a side agreement with the church's attorney, I was promised my job at the school and my salary. Years later I entered and won a lawsuit against the attorney for fraud. However, through a series of legal entanglements, I did not receive the proceeds from that settlement either.

In the months following my divorce, God always reassured me, "You're going to be OK." Like any newly single mom, I was worried. I fretted about being Marte Tilton in my late forties, starting from scratch. I felt that Christian "ministry" in general did not accept me. I felt that pastors ran from me. What would I ever do?

At first it hurt even to drag myself to work at the school and see the church across the street. It was devastating to watch them pull the dumpster up to the back door of the church and start pitching everything with my name, face or voice on it. But since that time, I have met so many people who have been so grateful for what they learned there. I believe God did a great work in that church while it stood.

Back to Divorce Court

Little more than two years after my own divorce, my husband divorced

31

his second wife. Their divorce was splashed across all the local newspapers on and off for about two years. In my divorce decree, a phrase read that if personal assets or money existed that I did not know about, then I would receive 90 percent of them. But I discovered through the newspapers that my ex-husband's second wife was trying to take millions of dollars in church assets. She had started transferring assets to the name of a church she was starting, claiming she could do so because she was a "copastor." But the assets were based on their divorce—which meant they must be personal in nature. I took action. I had forgiven them, but I did not want to allow church money to be turned to personal property and taken for personal gain.

Any lawsuit is totally consuming. Emotions, concern over what to say and worry about defending yourself are consuming. Before getting legally entangled even more while in the midst of all the other lawsuits, I kept asking the Lord what I should do. The scripture I heard in my heart was, "pursue, overtake and recover all." So I pursued.

When I walked into the courtroom with a lawyer, their faces became ashen. Because I did not want people to think I was selfishly going after church assets, I signed all my rights to that money over to the school, never dreaming that the money could possibly be unsafe in the hands of the school board. My interference forced a delay. They divorced without her receiving any of the church money. Because she had transferred some church property into her own name, which violated court orders, the newspapers said she ended up being fined a large amount, yet had received nothing. My case was never heard.

"TELL US HOW IT FEELS"

BEING CALLED TO BE A WITNESS IN A COURT CASE OR TO GIVE A DEPOSITION, which is also legal testimony, is trying at best and debilitating at worst. Starting in 1991, I have spent hours on the witness stand, given countless depositions and have learned to hold my emotions in check. Often I wanted to lash out, but aware that the lawyers were pushing me for that exact purpose, I have learned to keep myself under tight control. I actually became accustomed to testifying, but that is far from saying I was comfortable with it.

In January 1999 I was called to a hearing in a room filled with attorneys who were to argue before a judge as to whether the school we founded, which was all but defunct, could remain on church property. Ironically, I had resigned as director of the school eighteen months earlier in order to get on with my life.

On that cold January morning, I put on my navy blue suit, one of two that I always wore to court. Still today, when I wear one of those suits, my friends call me "The Defendant." As I headed for court, I noticed the oil light was still on in my car. The fact that I never carved out time to learn about cars has always seemed the least of my worries.

I sat on the witness stand in the judge's cramped courtroom in my blue defendant's suit as one of the church's lawyers questioned me unmercifully. Shouting, he demanded, "Tell us what it feels like to be thrown out of the school."

Every time I had been asked why I left the school, I had been forced to take a break so I could compose myself. It was such a tender spot in my heart because it had hurt so badly to leave the school. Often I would have to describe how—and why—the school parents or board members felt I was the problem.

What do my feelings have to do with the case? I wondered. *Why is the judge allowing that line of questioning? And why isn't my own lawyer objecting to his demeaning, sarcastic tone?* But I did not voice my questions. By this time I had learned to discipline myself and to stand firmly on the Word of God. Otherwise I would be led down a path where I did not need to go.

I had testified repeatedly that I *resigned* from the school—I had not been *fired*. Certainly I had been under a tremendous amount of pressure to leave. But the lawyers seemed to be looking for evidence that I was hiding something. I hid nothing.

But this lawyer just would not quit. He lit into me again and again—"Tell us how it feels!" I felt my composure begin to crumble. Finally, for the first and only time in all those hours and years of testimony, tears ran uncontrollably down my face. Trying to control the quiver in my voice as I spoke, I answered in a low voice, "It feels the same way it felt to be thrown out of my church."

I still have very mixed emotions about my legal decisions. I am grateful we did not embarrass the body of Christ even more by providing another media feeding frenzy. Yet, when I see what my children have gone through, not having the financial security that was once within my power to give them, it grieves me.

I found myself a single mom with few friends left. I had no church home, a shaky career as a school administrator and a soiled reputation. I was eventually stripped of all income as I fought the legal battles that still seem never to end.

I felt trapped in a bleak Charles Dickens' novel with every element except spontaneous human combustion. Soon I was standing in the middle of a mall, exposed to the world, trying to rebuild my life and make a living for my children by selling gift items such as stuffed bunnies from a kiosk. People stared, wondering if I was the real Marte Tilton.

But I realize now the biggest problem I faced was the terrible guilt that I had completely failed God. The heavens seemed shut up like brass to me, so I assumed it was because I had done something wrong.

At times I was so devastated that my life was reduced to two choices only: life or death. At those times, I clung to the belief that no matter how dark the tunnel in which I lived, at the end of that tunnel, God's light was shining for me.

> The only way out is through faith in Jesus Christ; the way of escape is open to all who believe him.
>
> —GALATIANS 3:22, TLB

There was certainly a way out provided for me—as there will be for you. In the following chapter, I will share what I learned that can help you avoid getting in such a huge mess in the first place!

CHAPTER 4

A SLIP INTO COMPROMISE

T O GET OUT OF TROUBLE, WE MUST LEARN HOW WE GOT INTO TROUBLE IN the first place. What took us there? What attracted trouble to us? No matter how dramatic our deliverance from trouble, if we do not know how we got there in the first place, we will end up in the same situation again. It took a lot of soul-searching and heart-probing for me to discover the roots of what went wrong in my life.

I can only speak for myself, and I refuse to surmise what was in hearts of those around me. My biggest issues were devastating to discover, and I have worked hard to get over feeling like a complete fool.

Satan never comes to tempt us with a huge dramatic sin first. He leads up to it by luring us into little compromises that seem insignificant at the time. His favorite lures are those that appear not only as if no one were hurt, but that also lead us to believe people were actually helped. That is how he ensnared me.

A CRACKED FOUNDATION

WITH ALL THAT WE DID RIGHT, THERE WAS PLENTY THAT WAS WRONG. ALTHOUGH there were cracks in our foundation, we launched venture after venture. If we did not make the necessary corrections, we would eventually fail—and fail we did. When the foundation finally crumbled, the resulting explosions destroyed the ministry, fractured our family and rocked the body of Christ. Many lives were hurt in the process, including men and women I know today who have never fully recovered from the pain they experienced. Many became embittered, and others simply lost their will to press on. It saddens me deeply to think of these precious people.

What were the mistakes? It sounds simplistic, but Satan has to start somewhere, and he chooses the little areas where temptation is easily disguised. It started for me when I became far too busy with "good works." In my busyness, I became compromised.

Compromise means "to blend." Christians who blend godly attributes with worldly attributes become confused and can then be deceived. *Compromise* can also be defined "to make a shameful or disreputable concession." Christians can certainly give in to a shameful way of believing and living when we compromise in any area of our lives. But this is very subtle.

The first step is to tolerate something. Next we accept it as normal, perhaps with a shrug, saying, "Oh well, this is what people do." Then we embrace it for ourselves. People with whom my husband and I surrounded ourselves were not always the most upright, nor did they have the best integrity. When we tolerated them, we fell very quickly into this pattern. Tolerate, accept, embrace.

THE TRAP

MY HUSBAND AND HIS VISION WERE FAR AHEAD OF THE TIMES. GOD INSPIRED him with things others could not imagine. He saw, for example, that one day people would have satellite dishes at their houses and could subscribe to the programming they wanted. The early dishes cost quite a bit, but a vendor gave a great discount to the people who joined the satellite network so they could buy their dishes at a bargain.

When we first started monthly satellite broadcasts, we asked only for offerings from the little rural churches that had no hope of hosting a major speaker. But when others saw what we were doing, they offered the same programming and did not request offerings. They said the gospel was free, and who could argue with that? They could afford to broadcast for free. At that time, we were still very much just a "mom-and-pop shop" that could not absorb such costs. Our satellite ministry consisted of a collection of several thousand churches who downlinked the monthly seminars that Word of Faith uplinked to satellite. Word of Faith paid for the seminar, TV equipment, crew, uplink satellite dish and satellite time. The churches only had to buy a satellite dish and send Word of Faith the offerings taken during the time they met to listen to the seminar. Then Bob had another idea—begin a twenty-four-hour satellite network.

Before launching the network, the pastors met with my husband in private meetings, which I did not attend, and asked him for some kind of an accountability structure. But my husband evidently would not submit to this. In fact, to the present day, I have heard about hard feelings due to these meetings and my husband's lack of accountability. I have been told I was kept in the dark on purpose, and I am still in the dark.

Pastors left our network. After all we had poured into their lives, that felt like a personal rejection. Against the better judgment of many on staff, including my own objections, we started a twenty-four-hour satellite network and tried to enlist the satellite pastors as part of it. This experience became a watershed experience—and I vowed that I would never again violate what I felt was right in my heart. The satellite network, which collapsed within three months, plunged us into a debt of over a million dollars.

That was when our ministry changed. The twenty-four-hour

network was a big disappointment for my husband. Some have observed he was never quite the same after it. But this was also when he made some new friends. Instead of the pastors and men who had been our friends before, he turned to others who, in my opinion, had something to gain from him but nothing to offer. His new friends were employees who could never have gotten away with as few hours or as little productivity elsewhere. Nor could they have disregarded policies and procedures elsewhere. His insistence on keeping these friends and my outspokenness about their character created an irreparable rift in our marriage.

I know he became depressed. Members of the staff and I encouraged him to take some time off to rest following the network disaster. But when he returned from a trip alone to Hawaii, he came home with a new idea about telling people to pay their "vows," which he preached extensively for years after.

The collapse of the twenty-four-hour network and the resulting debt may or may not have been a turning point for us—each of us chose our own path. No matter what anyone else did or thought, I decided to follow my conscience. This got me in trouble over the next few years with people around me who confused following my conscience with outright rebellion. With the improved vision of hindsight that I have today, I disagree with their complaints even more strongly now than I did at the time. But one thing almost everyone got right was that as I dug my heels in, I became a workaholic—determined to do my part to make things work.

I will never forget fighting those financial battles and trying to be strong for others when we were so deeply in debt. I would have my faithful friend Phyllis, who was the accounting manager, print out the checks that were due to vendors. Then I would decide which ones could be sent. As I prayed about it, I felt God telling me just to do what I could do each day. Desperately wanting to be rid of the mountain of debt incurred by the satellite network's collapse, as well as with a devastating loss from postal workers stealing our mail, I did everything I could to hold it all together. Phyllis and I would even bring in the bills and literally turn on the audiocassette tape player of Kenneth Hagin, Sr. teaching on *"El Shaddai,* the God Who Is More Than Enough." I do not know what method worked best, but I do know God was merciful—the mountain of debt diminished, and soon we were back on our feet financially.

I thought I was doing so well. I thought I was behaving so heroically, saving the day. I thought I was doing what was best for others, which is the most subtle and insidious kind of compromise Satan can lure us into. It was a snare.

I did not fully understand it then, and I do not fully understand it now, but I figured if Bob was sick and depressed, I had better work harder. I comforted him as best I could at home, then went to work, where I covered for him, telling people he was too sick to be there. The time came when he only preached two Sundays a month; I handled the rest.

Out of care and concern for a sick spouse—and not a small case of codependence—I became the family provider, protector and caretaker. If my husband wanted to show up only for his television program, I said, "Not a problem," and covered for him. If he wanted to leave town for some rest and recreation, "Not a problem." I would cover for him. When there was a negative issue to deal with at church, I was the one who confronted it. I was so concerned about keeping everything going, ensuring it was perfectly legal and done with a great degree of excellence, that I just kept adding to my own work, which took me down a path I would rather not have traveled.

In addition to becoming the caretaker, I inadvertently became my husband's "mother," and not a very good one at that. While I was running around "busy about my Father's business"—or so I thought—my husband was building a new life for himself, one about which I knew nothing. I made horrible mistakes, all clothed in "good works," and disregarded the cracks in the foundation that were readily apparent. Although I continued my daily time in God's Word early each day, instead of pressing into Him, I just got busier with the demands to do a good job. Regardless of media attention, satellite networks, lawsuits or anything else, we were headed for a fall—not caused from without, but from within.

I tolerated my husband's disrespect, accepting it as my lot in life, but when I was asked to embrace the compromise I saw around me, I fought back. I could tolerate and accept, but I could not embrace. By the time I had gone that far, it was too late. He wanted things his way, and he knew how to get it. If I got in the way, I had to be dealt with. By the time *PrimeTime Live* aired, my husband had not needed me for quite some time. Yet I needed so much to be needed that I saw none of this accumulating over the years.

Because my husband told me he loved me every day, I never felt completely unloved. I felt that I should "stand by my man," never recognizing that I was enabling him to fall further into questionable patterns.

I never compromised financially or in any legal sense—far from it as can be seen from the rules we lived by—but I did compromise. I overbusied myself with good works because it seemed right at the time. Driving forces within the heart are often unknown to us. The Bible says only God knows what is truly in our hearts, and we have to ask Him to show us. Guilt planted in the heart is an incredible force, as are greed, pride, bitterness, fear and shame.

Regardless of any internal pressures I faced, it was my decision to make some compromises that proved to be bad decisions. Going through the list of ways I compromised is a lengthy road, and we could take a long walk down it, but it serves no purpose. Yet compromise is important to discover because of the snowball effect it has. In no way could I have imagined the mess into which it would plunge me.

THE FATHER'S HOUSE

THE LIFE OF JOSEPH IS ENORMOUSLY INSPIRING TO ME BECAUSE HE NAIVELY FELL into messes just as I did. Joseph had a dream when he was about seventeen years old that God would promote him and favor him above his family. In his youth and naivete, he expected his family to rejoice when he told them. Instead, his father became somewhat indignant, and his brothers immediately tried to bring him down. When they encountered him away from his father's protection, they beat him, threw him in a pit and sold him to slave traders wandering through their country. Once in Egypt, Joseph was sold to a wealthy man whose wife led him into a seductive trap, which he fled. As a result, she had him imprisoned indefinitely. What could Joseph do in prison? The same thing he had done in the pit and on the slave route—work on the condition of his own heart.

I was much like Joseph, naively caught up in being God's "ambassador," while others dug a pit for me, which I blindly fell into. People say I always come across as a self-confident, strong woman, but inside I am still a shy country girl who simply tried to be a good ambassador. Like Joseph, when I stepped away from my Father's protection, the enemy was able to move in and crush me. In no way did Joseph understand this or expect what was coming. Although God gave me inklings of what was to come, I did not understand the clues either.

In the early eighties, I had a dream of driving up to the church property and seeing no cars in the parking lot. I later saw that dream realized. I could not imagine it at the time, and because the dream made me fearful, I thought it was not of God. In 1981, God spoke to me that I would "be as Joseph." I did not understand that either. The church was only five years old. Being young in the Lord and innocently believing that life was brimming with endless possibilities of blessings, I just figured I needed to rebuke the devil more.

I know the "curse causeless" does not come. (See Proverbs 26:2.) I have learned that we can know someone and be known by them—but only to the degree we both allow ourselves to be known. Sometimes it takes a while to figure out who people really are. They can sound good, but we do not know what is in their hearts. I do not know what was in my husband's heart, nor would I surmise that now. But looking back, I think a fundamental shift occurred way back in the early eighties. I simply cannot, to this day, identify what it was.

The principles taught by Edwin Louis Cole have been a great part of God's restoration in my life. Dr. Cole says, "Your talent can take you places that your character cannot maintain." Perhaps our wells were not dug deeply enough; we had not developed our character sufficiently. We could have been too inexperienced for all we attempted, or we tried to grow too quickly. Whatever it may have been, the *PrimeTime Live* telecast did not destroy the ministry. The seeds of destruction had already been planted, and it was only a matter of time until that crop began to come up.

The prodigal son of Luke 15 went into a foreign land. He wanted to make his mark on the world, but he ended up living with pigs. He did not belong in that foreign land—he did not know how to live there. In the same way, we do not belong where we do not belong. Way back then, I thought that disobeying my heart, even a little, was just between God and me. Never once did it cross my mind that within seemingly "innocent" compromises were seeds of death that could affect not just those around me, but also thousands of others who suffered the embarrassment and humiliation of seeing us fall.

Our "land" is our own heart—the hidden springs of our mental and emotional activities. The foreign land that ensnared the prodigal is for us whatever causes us to violate what we know to be right in our heart. Jesus said that evil things come out of the heart and defile the entire person (Matt. 15:19–20). Our land needs to be reconditioned after everything around us dies. Everything I ever did successfully, outside of mothering my children, died. My marriage, my church, my relationships, my reputation, my career—all died. A piece of my heart seemed to die with each one. But God's resurrection power binds up our broken hearts and makes us whole.

When I entered what seemed like a dark tunnel, I wanted so much to feel God's pleasure again, to be in His house. For years, every day I had known that what I was doing was what God wanted me to do. It was a wonderful place to be. I strayed far away from the person God created me to be. But God restored me. Five years after being forced out of my church, I returned to full-time service with another ministry. The enemy had convinced me I was utterly unworthy of being a servant of the Lord. But ministry is where I thrive. This is my "land"— where my heart is.

When the Word is not planted in our hearts, we will not see it grow up into a successful crop. We may know the Word in our minds, yet not agree with God in our hearts. God said that in the last days, He would "put My law in their minds, and write it on their hearts" (Jer. 31:33, NKJV). These are those days. His Word is the seed we must plant in our "land."

I encourage you today to plant and nurture the good seed of His Word—no matter what you are facing. Do not compromise your heart!

FIGHT OR FLIGHT?

LIKE ANIMALS, HUMANS HAVE WHAT SCIENTISTS CALL THE "FIGHT-OR-FLIGHT instinct." We can become angry, touchy, fretful, blame others and even turn against the ones we love or those who love us. We can wear ourselves out with lawsuits, debates, meetings or

44

even a new drive to succeed in hope of showing the offenders how wrong they were.

In "flight" mode, however, we want to run. We want to hide, cover up, seclude ourselves and live in denial. Some people in distress do run, uprooting everything to move as far away as possible. Others develop a "persecution complex," becoming victims and easily victimized. Some blame God for their troubles and run back to the life of a sinner. Many cry out, "Why?" "Where did I go wrong?" "Who would do such a horrible thing to me?" Expressing those emotions can be healthy, but if we linger there, the victim mentality sets in.

Others hide by withdrawing, believing everything is about them. They become self-centered, self-consumed and wallow in self-pity, which is a form of idolizing ourselves. (See Galatians 5:19–21.) The enemy loves for us to withdraw into seclusion, because once he gets us alone, he can utterly destroy us.

Or we can become filled with shame, accepting the wrongs of others as our own fault. A husband loses his job, and the wife suffers. Parents divorce, and the children suffer. A pastor leaves, and the church suffers. An employee quits, and the boss suffers. It happens on all levels.

"Flight" for me included the belief that in order to avoid the pain I should move—although I could not afford it. I used some of my divorce settlement to pay the attorney, some as a down payment on a house and its furnishings, some for moving expenses and some to pay our expenses for our hotel stay while waiting for the house to be completed. I even used some to keep the school afloat. I put the rest into a CD that could be used for my children and me to live off if I did not get a paycheck for some reason.

People still ask me why I stayed in Dallas. When it came down to it, I simply did not want to run. I did not want to give credibility to the false allegations in the newspapers and on television. Many other things were wrong, but the ones named in the media were not. Besides, my children and I had already moved to California once, and we did not want to leave home again.

Another option we entertained was to change our name. My children and I talked about this frequently. My two youngest were in the church's grade school at the time and somewhat protected, but my two oldest were in college when our name was emblazoned across headlines almost daily. People mocked their last name. But the children finally decided that to change their name was akin to denying their parentage, so they decided against it. It was just as well. Everyone knew my face. I remember sitting in a restaurant when one of the patrons walked up and said, "Your husband is a lowdown blankity-blank..." I said, "I'm sorry you feel that way, Sir." Changing my name would not have solved that problem!

Still today I am asked, "Are you any relation to Robert Tilton?"

I always respond, "Yes, I was the first wife, married to him for twenty-five years."

Some people find an "emergency exit" by pretending the problem does not exist. If they are Christians, they may even call their denial "faith." Instead of praying God's Word over the situation, they believe the situation will simply go away. Or they just numb themselves—ranging from physical addictions such as food to movie and sports addictions and even to drugs and alcohol.

God could have provided His own "emergency exit" in the form of a miracle to deliver me. But He did not do so. God's Word never promises that trials and troubles will not happen. But His Word does promise that He will be with us in the midst of them.

> Thou hast caused men to ride over our heads; we went through fire and through water; but thou broughtest us out into a wealthy place.
>
> —Psalm 66:12

God did bless me a hundredfold in many ways, just as He promised in November 1974. But sometimes we forget that along with the promise of the hundredfold come the words "with persecutions" (Mark 10:30). We do not want to believe that if we are obedient to God, we can still have disasters and crises. Yet committed Christians are being persecuted all over the globe today.

My family was not persecuted for the sake of righteousness. The early Christians were persecuted because they followed Christ, cast out demons, healed on the Sabbath and did other righteous acts—not because they had too many houses and the church they led had become "big business" in the eyes of society. What was implanted in our hearts that could have brought on a mess like that? I have certainly looked down that dark well, and I have been disappointed at what I found. Although we were not guilty of the charges levied against us, there were other areas where we were not living according to God's standards.

CHAPTER 5

THE WEB OF DECEPTION

C OMPROMISE IS AN OPEN ROAD TO DECEPTION. DECEPTION RISES FROM the confused shadows of a compromised heart. When we are deceived, we forget who we are. We become disoriented, lose our bearings and lose our sense of time or identity. *Deception* means "to accept as true or valid what is false or invalid." I have heard several ministers call this simply "winking at sin." I think I have seen some people "wink" until both eyes are shut—tight.

Jesus said:

> For from within, out of men's hearts, come evil thoughts, sexual immorality, theft, murder, adultery, greed, malice, deceit, lewdness, envy, slander, arrogance and folly.
> —MARK 7:21–22, NIV

Deception excuses what comes from the heart. Deception comes from at least three directions. We can deceive ourselves, venturing so far into denial that we believe our own lies. We can be deceived by others or caught up in their deception and delusion. And we can be deceived spiritually by Satan, as the spiritual blight that comes from an impure heart creeps into our minds.

I found myself out of the will of God through compromise, which led to confusion, which led to deception. But I found myself back into the will of God by repentance.

> Search me, O God, and know my heart: try me, and know
> my thoughts: and see if there be any wicked way in me.
> —PSALM 139:23–24

Repentance is not a once-and-for-all exercise that we do to receive salvation. Repentance is a lifestyle of devotion to God, covering our sins with the blood of Jesus and, by His grace, living each day for Him.

ROAD SIGNS ON THE PATH TO DESTRUCTION

DOWNFALLS DO NOT COME SUDDENLY. SOLOMON'S LIFE ERODED. CHARLES Swindoll teaches that Solomon's downfall was due to:

- Unwise alliance with unbelievers—1 Kings 3:1. He was always marrying new wives to form political alliances. This could have been due to lust or the fear of man.

- Unholy involvement with idolatry—1 Kings 3:2–3. When the temple was built, the high places were not torn down. Preoccupation with "things" is just another form of idolatry.

- Unresolved conflicts with a friend—1 Kings 9:10–14. Solomon entered an agreement with King Hiram to provide building supplies. He cheated King Hiram and never made it right.

- Unrestrained preoccupation with sex—1 Kings 11:1–8. Sensual gratification became a downfall when his wives and concubines turned his heart toward other gods.

Solomon's affections toward God did not change overnight. He never rejected God completely, but he ignored God and refused to be held accountable (1 Kings 11:6). Solomon heard from the Lord three times: First, in a beautiful time of fellowship when God gave him wisdom. Second, when he dedicated the temple and God cautioned him not to turn away. The third time was when Solomon's heart had turned, and God said his sons would lose the kingdom.

Moses had already decreed that the king must not accumulate many wives or much wealth for himself (Deut. 17:17). Solomon willingly defied the written law and God's verbal warnings, dabbling in sin, amassing wealth and pursuing companionships with the ungodly. Solomon also turned to "strange" women, marrying many foreign brides. Yet, in Proverbs, he advises us to avoid the "strange" woman. Imagine his outcome had he taken his own advice to heart![1]

Like Solomon, when we accept something foreign to God's kingdom, it can seduce us and lead us into deeper deception. This slow process is going on all around us in varying degrees, to the point that it is sometimes hard to tell Christians apart from the world. We dabble in what we know is wrong—whether provocative television, Internet porn or compromising fashions. We justify ourselves with the excuse that "we're not *hurting* anyone." We watch each other's actions instead of keeping our eyes on Jesus and accepting His Word as our guide. We see someone we respect going into a questionable movie, so we think, *I must just be a prude,* and soon we are going into that movie as well.

Any seemingly innocent exploration can start a downfall. It always starts small and never seems that it could possibly take us down a path to destruction. Then one day we find ourselves divorced, in financial ruin or with rebellious kids, and we wonder what happened. It is our hearts that turn from God first.

A PROTECTED LIFE

As THE CHURCH GREW LARGE, CERTAIN INDIVIDUALS WERE ATTRACTED BY THE crowds, and we felt threatened by some of their bizarre behavior. By 1988 we were receiving death threats. People would come to our home unannounced and uninvited for uncertain purposes. The bomb threats and death threats did not really scare me, but I could not abide the thought that innocent church members might be sitting in a service and have a bomb go off—or the thought that something I could have prevented might happen to one of my children.

The only time I remember being truly fearful for our safety was at a crusade in Brazil in mid-1980 when an appreciative mob shook our car and we thought it might tip over. All things considered, we decided to have security measures employed, which seemed prudent, but which also meant we would have people around us all the time.

On the surface it appears nice to have people at your beck and call so you do not have to worry about anything because others take care of everything. Your car is always clean and filled with gas and oil because aides, secretaries and assistants anticipate your needs. For a time we had someone who would pick up our kids from school and help me in the home. On the surface, it was ideal. But below the surface, it worked to strengthen deception, which was disastrous.

I doubt people realize how much influence they carry with the people they are called to serve. The last thing a preacher needs is a security officer criticizing the sermon as he steps off the platform, an assistant asking for advice or, because they "see everything," talking about their employers behind their backs. It is logical that people who do those things are usually fired. Those who keep their jobs inadvertently become "yes men," even if all they intend is to be encouraging. The loyal, levelheaded employee who loves his or her job and can interact without falling into flattery is a rare jewel.

I have seen people with entourages who act like stars. I did not set out to be a star, but that is how we were often treated. Security people kept everyone at arm's length from us. Our closest friends, people who came up with us in the ministry, could no longer get close to us. We would have to tell the security guards, "He's OK, I want to talk to him."

I remember our head usher, David Lovell, his lovely wife, Linda and their family, who were a deep part of our roots and are still some of my closest friends. When another friend told me of a crisis David and Linda were facing, I visited them and was astonished to discover they had been unable to get through to me because of security guards who stopped them and secretaries who thought I should not be bothered with their calls. We often did not ask for this screening, but employees assumed they knew whom we wanted to see or speak to, so they chose who would or would not get through. That is a management problem, and a difficult one to tackle.

When we moved to California in 1988, for the first time we bought a home in a gated community to maintain some privacy. Sometimes those gates are for prestige, but we felt we needed the security they offered. Undetected, "fear of man" was taking hold on our minds.

Even with employees all around us, people would still get through. We would often have strange visits. I woke up one morning to find a black briefcase on the porch. Call security. One night we found a man with a gun outside. Call security. Once our yard was papered with Monopoly money. When we lived on a golf course, daily we heard the shouts of golfers yelling "Fraud"—and worse—across our fence. Often the golf balls that broke our windows seemed to have been something other than missed shots. These pranks were not pulled by juvenile delinquents, but by well-to-do businessmen who I was surprised would subject my children to such antics.

Then there were the helicopters. From the time the media investigations first started in Dallas before the *PrimeTime Live* telecast, our house was buzzed continually by helicopters. Even when we were no longer living in the home in California, aerial photos of that house were splashed all over local and national news reports about us. At our home in Dallas, the helicopters always brought bad news. When I heard them overhead, I knew to tune in that night to the local news. For certain, some angle on the story was being pursued. Along with the lawyers or plaintiffs they were interviewing would be my husband's face or aerial views of our home.

The fear that creeps into the mind is a trap. While I protected my children's physical well-being, I inadvertently allowed something equally dangerous to attack their spiritual well-being. My two youngest were aghast after the divorce when we moved into an unprotected housing tract. My kids had developed an attitude that *something* was *out there*—and it wanted to get us. Jesus said, "Fear not them which kill the body, but are not able to kill the soul; but rather fear him which is able to destroy both soul and body in hell" (Matt. 10:28).

I can understand people having security systems, but giving in to the fear of man rather than having faith in God is a snare. "Fearing people is a dangerous trap, but to trust the LORD means safety" (Prov. 29:25, NLT).

> For God hath not given us the spirit of fear; but of power,
> and of love, and of a sound mind.
> —2 TIMOTHY 1:7

When we remove fear, we have power, love and a sound mind. But when we give in to fear, it overtakes a sound mind, removes our power and hinders our ability to act in love. That's the trap!

THE FEAR OF MAN

SOLOMON MADE COVENANTS WITH OTHER KINGS BY MARRYING THEIR DAUGHTERS in order to be politically protected from attack. He walked in fear of enemies, not faith in God. By fearing them, he made his enemies to be bigger than God. Abraham made the same mistake when he gave Sarah to a foreign king in order to ensure he would be safe when he entered foreign territory. "You pretend to be my sister so I won't get hurt," he said in essence. And he did it *twice!* (See Genesis 12:10–20; 20.)

Becoming afraid that circumstances are too big for God to handle is one of the temptations we face when we rise to a new level of prosperity or responsibility. We can feel it when we buy our first car, manage our first employee or make our first million. The higher you move, the higher the stakes—and the greater the temptation to fear.

Fear can create reactions such as striking out or running from people, instead of embracing and trying to help people. This is why many leaders do not interact with people in the same way they did when they were coming up. Not just ministers, but politicians, singers and actors—anyone in the public eye—can isolate themselves due to fear.

To overcome fear, grab hold of the Word of God. Fear God— not man. Every morning I pray my own paraphrase of Psalm 91:

> Because we fear the LORD the angels of the LORD encamp about us to keep us safe. No evil shall befall us, nor will any calamity come near us or our dwelling. He alone is our refuge, our place of safety. He shields us with His wings. His faithful promises are our armor and protection, and He orders His angels wherever we go.

DECEPTION ENTERED OUR MARRIAGE

IN ALL OUR EFFORTS TO DO WHAT WE THOUGHT WAS GOOD AND RIGHT, MY husband and I fell into traps that seem obvious to me now. By

1985, when our last precious son was born, the ministry had thoroughly wedged itself in front of the family as a priority. This is common for business people, ministers and fathers, as well as mothers. We visit Sister So-and-so in the hospital instead of watching our son play soccer. We start planning the family calendar around the business or ministry. Ministers get the attitude that family will always be there, so they can catch up with kids and spouses later. Those are seeds of destruction that will reap a bitter crop.

In marriage, the enemy plays off our weaknesses to trick us and cheat us if we do not pay attention. When a marriage partner gets off balance, the strengths of the other begin to appear bothersome and may seem like an "irreconcilable difference" for which the marriage should dissolve. Divorce is not the answer. Getting back on track is the answer.

My husband began to allow others to forget that I was called into ministry alongside him. Pastors' wives often become the scapegoat. Church members think they can say anything to the pastor's wife if her husband does. I have heard ministers say from the pulpit things like, "Sarah called Abraham 'lord,' so when you are going to start that, Honey?" I have also seen leaders come home from ministering and expect their wives to fall all over them as the people did where they ministered. But she is picking up his dirty socks, watching his bad habits and saying, "You're still the same man I married." The role of family is always to provide balance for us in one way or another against the imbalance of the outside world—not to go along with that imbalance. We would not expect our families to join in slandering us. Likewise we should not expect them to join in pampering us.

Because of my work today, I read personal letters from all over the world, and I know these attitudes and issues are an epidemic. If a man is truly accepting his responsibility as the head of the family, he is doing for his family what Christ does for the church. Any leader's first responsibility—whether in business or ministry, male or female—is always to his or her family.

I went way overboard trying to serve my husband. But I finally drew the line where it violated my heart. Our own conscience with God must not be violated because of devotion to a spouse or from a perverted sense of "submission." This is particularly true with lust. People sitting in the pews have real-life problems with husbands involved in Internet pornography and wives flirting with other men. These people hear the preacher quoting from the Word that our body is not our own and that the marriage bed is undefiled. So one spouse violates his or her conscience while trying to hang on to the other, instead of dealing with the root problem, which is lust. They feel horrid for being a party to the others' lust, but they cannot find help or a clear understanding of God's Word. The solution goes back to what we are sowing and reaping in our own hearts.

When we are the spouse being pushed to the edge or beyond the limits of our conscience, we can begin to view ourselves as the other views us. "You are a nag." "You are a prude." "You're fat." "You'll never change." If Satan can twist the Word so we believe the accusations are justified, we develop a high tolerance for inappropriate behavior.

But I got myself into it. In the self-sufficient frame of mind into which I fell, I decided I could take care of myself. Eventually, when my husband wanted a divorce, I thought I would just do what I had always done and I would be fine. But I was not fine. Once we divorced, nothing I did that I had done before worked. I had to humble myself to remember that without God blessing my life, nothing would ever work.

I had to take a long, realistic look at my heart to see that, in spite of my efforts, it had become polluted. The Lord said, "Let none deal treacherously against the wife of his youth. . . . Ye have wearied the LORD with your words" (Mal. 2:15, 17). We weary the Lord when we complain about our spouse or ex-spouse. We weary the Lord when we say, "Every one that doeth evil is good in the sight of the LORD" (v. 17). We weary Him when we say, "Where is the God of judgment?" (v. 17). It wearies the Lord to suggest He has put His stamp of approval on wrongdoing. God cannot bless evil.

The curse comes in many ways and for many reasons, but the curse we can completely avoid is found in Deuteronomy 28:47–48:

> Because you did not serve the Lord your God with joy-fulness of [mind and] heart [in gratitude] for the abundance of all [with which He had blessed you], therefore you shall serve your enemies whom the Lord shall send against you...
>
> —AMP

If we do not obey God we will suffer the curse. But if we obey the voice of the Lord our God, we will be blessed. Even if we go through the fire, we will not be burned or even smell like smoke, and eventually we will be delivered.

Whatever you may have done to bring on the curse, no matter how justified you feel—or even if you were simply the "victim" of another's actions—remember that sin is sin. We cannot expect to get on with our lives without accepting responsibility for our own sins, and we cannot get on with life when we are accepting responsibility for the sins of others.

BE CAREFUL OF UNWISE ASSOCIATIONS

IN THE CONFUSION OF COMPROMISE AND THE CONSTANT ACTIVITY, PEOPLE befriended us whom we should have never let in. One minister "friend" preached a doctrine of "grace." According to him, you could live as you wanted, do what you wanted and God would forgive you. But you could never step down from the pulpit because the "gifts and callings of God are without repentance" (Rom. 11:29). What a perversion of Scripture! God will never leave us, never abandon us. But if we leave Him, it is time to step down from leadership! Yet this minister's dogmas were just pebbles in the shoe compared to other things allowed in.

Television people tend to exude "hype," offering to make ordinary people into "stars." All of a sudden we found ourselves in television makeup, looking pretty and singing like birds, which seemed nice. Television people need to make a living. The way most do this is to make someone think they are something they are not—which, in a word, is "great." Tolerating, then accepting and finally embracing such people was one of our worst errors.

Other people were also opportunistic or had hidden agendas we never discerned. Someone within our office reported us to the IRS. We had received poor advice early in ministry, which we diligently corrected once we learned the laws. But their letter to the IRS resulted in our first mini-audit. Fortunately we passed that audit with flying colors because by then we were squeaky clean.

The majority of our congregation and staff was made up of faithful students of God's Word who served Him with their whole hearts, but I often could not see them for the few who brought so much grief. We caught people in the accounting department stealing from the church, so we moved our accounting operations to a bank recommended by our lawyer. Some staff members committed adultery. People in our Outstanding Young Americans program fell into various forms of sin. Leaders whom we trained turned on us and said bad things about us. And at least a half dozen times we caught ushers stealing from the offering plates.

I felt let down each time. But when I expressed my disappointment, I was accused of demanding perfection. Instead of confronting, we often ended up tolerating, accepting and eventually embracing what others did. Disappointment leads to disillusionment, which can lead to bitterness or cynicism. I desperately tried to fight a huge case of cynicism. *Cynicism* is simply believing that others are motivated only by self-interest.

Pastor A. R. Bernard teaches that when we are cynical or bitter, we can fall into any kind of unethical or immoral behavior. (See Ecclesiastes 2:20–24.) He tells the story of two partners in business. One partner did all the work while the other golfed, yet they divided the profits evenly. The working partner became so angry and cynical about the nonworking partner that he began to take more than his fair share. Because he had brought it all in, he felt justified in taking more. Thank God, we never fell beyond cynicism or bitterness. We would have been roasted.

Instead, lawyers told us what we could and could not do with our finances and with the finances of the church. After following all advice to avoid government intervention, we were investigated by all agencies, including paying taxes to the state comptroller for items sold in our bookstore.

If I wanted to make a contribution to something my children took part in, I was not allowed to do so because there I had a private interest. We could not have a bookstore because it was an open door for the government to come in. It seemed that for everything we tried to do for all the right reasons, there were a hundred legal reasons not to do it. Because the church was incorporated, we were prisoners to the corporation. It often seemed crazy, but we followed every single rule, which is why we were never even found with the reasonable suspicion of a crime. We had gone so overboard and been so nitpicky, that even with us sitting under a microscope for several years, no reasonable suspicion surfaced for any of the many government agencies to press charges.

When it is time to rest, we need to back off and rest. Think, pray and talk things through, even if your momentum dies a little. Trust God to revive it and show you the way. The time it took for me to dig out of the mess was many hundred times longer than what it would have taken to be refreshed with a Sabbath—and the results were so much worse.

THE FLATTERING TONGUE

DECEPTION SETTLED OVER OUR MINISTRY LIKE A THICK BLANKET, AND NO MATTER how good or how godly, it seemed no one was immune. With eight hundred employees rocked by a national exposé and leaders who were falling into disagreement, loyalties wavered. Probably seven hundred ninety of those employees were the salt of the earth. But all it took were the few who were not.

Many months after the *PrimeTime Live* television program, papers landed on my desk one morning with proof that one of our staff members had been caught by the police in a lewd act—and the story was headed for the newspapers. I knew the man well because he had ingratiated himself to my husband. I talked to my husband, who said, "It didn't happen the way the police said."

Skeptical, I talked to one of the church's lawyers who had talked with the employee. He said simply, "It was a setup," and refused to address the issues. With all the evidence in the world to the contrary, it appeared they were happy to compromise for the employee and sell the deception to the rest of the staff.

Solomon was decorated, lauded and exalted by his own people as well as by the kings and queens around him. King Hiram of Tyre sang his praises. The Queen of Sheba declared his wonders. He was considered the greatest king of all time. (See 1 Kings 4:30–34.) But Solomon became aware that people were flattering him.

Probably all organizations deal with people who ingratiate themselves to the leaders in order to be promoted, get a raise or get away with something. *To ingratiate* means "to disarm, please, flatter, seduce or coax." *To flatter* is "to praise excessively, especially from motives of self interest." *Flattery* is also defined as "a pleasing self-deception." Living the lifestyle of a leader,

people start saying things like, "Look at all God has blessed y
with." "You're doing great." "You're worth it." "You deserve it." It is
easy to start thinking *you* made everything happen—*not God.*

Solomon taught us to distrust flatterers.

> Meddle not with him that flattereth with his lips.... A
> flattering mouth worketh ruin.... A man that flattereth his
> neighbour spreadeth a net for his feet.
>
> —PROVERBS 20:19; 26:28; 29:5

Daniel said men are able to obtain the whole kingdom by
flattery. (See Daniel 11:21.) Some people who received their
income through their association with us felt they had to ingratiate themselves to ensure they kept their jobs. I know I heard
flatterers, talebearers and gossips, and I am sure my husband
heard even more. By tolerating it, we gave it a gateway and a
foothold. The flattering "seductress" whom Solomon described
in his proverbs is not just a woman—it is anything that seduces,
and it can cost you your life.

> So she seduced him with her pretty speech. With her flat-
> tery she enticed him.... He was like a bird flying into a
> snare, little knowing it would cost him his life.
>
> —PROVERBS 7:21, 23, NLT

Solomon discovered that a seductress was more bitter than
death and that sinners would be caught in her snare. We are
never above temptation. For every temptation we overcome,
more await us. We can be tempted in just about anything—
becoming proud of how much we pray, feeling sufficient in ourselves to accomplish God's will, coveting someone's car in the
church parking lot.

The seducer can be someone or something that sounds
religious: "I have peace offerings with me; this day have I
payed my vows" (Prov. 7:14). Flatterers can make you believe
you are the most important person on earth. "Therefore came

ee, diligently to seek thy face, and I have decked my bed with coverings of tapestry, with fine linen of Egypt...Come, let us ⊔ı love until the morning" (vv. 15–18).

⊔y mid-1980, bizarre incidents cropped up, some of which I am certain were unfounded, but it gave one cause to wonder about the kinds of people with whom we were associating. For example, a young man in our Bible college was investigated by the FBI for dealing guns illegally.

My husband always traveled with other men, so I never worried about him. But what were those men doing? I do not know to the present day, but I realize now there were opportunities when a question or two about the truth could have burst into my conscious mind. In the confusion of compromise, the busyness of good works and with my natural naivete, I was easily deceived. His friends, although involved in ministry as he was, were gradually pulling him further and further away from not only his family, but from his godly lifestyle as well.

One new associate had come to our ministry after the downfall of another major ministry. He was handsome and spoke with a silver tongue, and he quickly infiltrated the network of associates surrounding us and ingratiated himself to my husband. But rumors of impure and immoral activities seemed to follow him. I closed my eyes and ears to such rumors, but I have learned in recent years that even my children had been confronted with the evidence of this immorality.

Another friend was more sinister and direct with his attempts to pull Bob into questionable directions, particularly with his perverted views that God's grace would cover anything a minister did. His manipulative tactics—as well as those of my husband's other associates—began to isolate my husband from other more positive associations—including myself. He "preached" to him continually about my unsubmissive, legalistic attitudes, claiming that I was interfering with God's call on my husband's life.

Both these friends blamed my legalistic policies in the ministry when they were unable to immediately purchase expensive equipment and institute new programs. My husband and I argued about the influence of these friends continually.

Not until the days surrounding my 1993 divorce did I begin to see clearly the magnitude of what these people had done or the low levels to which their minds gravitated. And I am still discovering the effects this chaotic season of our lives had upon my family.

Deception Is a Downward Spiral

THE DECEPTION I HAD FALLEN FOR CAME TO AN END WHEN MY MARRIAGE ENDED, but for others it picked up momentum. A few months after my divorce, probably in early 1994, the congregation was introduced to a new doctrine coming from a group in North Carolina that believed Christians were filled with devils and needed to wail aloud every day to remove them.

The congregation was well schooled from years of studying the Word of God. My husband had continually told them for almost twenty years, "Don't take my word for it. Study the Word for yourself." They did. What a mess came as faithful members bucked the new doctrine. I was fighting my own battles across the street at the school with the lawyers closing in on me, but I became a sounding board for many congregation members and friends who were tossed about by the doctrines preached at the church.

From what I heard from congregation members and staff members, the wailers took the expensive puppets and marvelous toys we had bought for our children's church and threw them all away, claiming they had devils.

The staff was ordered, and the church members were "encouraged," to go to sessions to learn the new doctrine at a building we had bought across the freeway for Christian training. They sat in straight-backed chairs and listened to long lectures about wailing. Then the wailing would start, and what a commotion the congregation members described. One said she would sing "The Star-Spangled Banner" at the top of her lungs instead of participating in that travesty, but no one ever heard her above the din. I could always tell by their raspy voices when someone had been in a wailing service.

In one report, as the staff size dwindled, remaining staff members were divided into groups of ten. Their chairs were arranged in circles, and the groups were instructed to wail together as a group and pound each other on the back. In the center of the circles, discarded offering buckets had been placed to catch the exorcised demons.

Many stayed because, like me, they could not believe that after all we had been through together, it was all going to end like this. They kept praying for the day their pastor would return to the principles he had taught them. Many of the godly leaders of the church banded together and wrote a doctrinal statement that criticized the new teaching. I still have a copy of their work, which was inspired and anointed. But they could not convince their pastor that he was in error. Disillusioned members steadily left the church because of the new teachings that came in.

The church was still over a thousand strong, with the faithful clinging to the hope that it would turn around. A few hundred faithfully stayed on and were in attendance the day my ex-husband introduced his new wife. By the time he divorced her a year later, he told me by telephone that he was ready to "divorce" the wailing doctrine as well. By then the church was a shadow of what it had formerly been. Only a handful of people remained.

NO ONE IS IMMUNE

WE ARE ALL CAPABLE OF BEING SEDUCED. IF SOMEONE SAYS YOU ARE THE greatest, offers you a meal and a new set of clothes, you might fall into it. Someone else might not fall until they are offered a Rolex watch as well. For another it may be fame. For some it is a marriage. For Adam and Eve, it was a beautiful, sweet piece of fruit.

Satan carefully selects "sweet fruit" to suit our personalities and capitalize on our weaknesses. As we resist each "sweet fruit" offered, Satan increases the shine to offer it again, or he comes up with something new. But these temptations are merely tests that, when passed, serve to strengthen our faith, not destroy it.

I have been in churches in the same vicinity of where my ex-husband and I pastored, and I have cringed when pastors said things like, "I'm not going to be like the fellow down the street," referring to my ex-husband. Thinking you are above the seduction, the temptation and the allure of sin is the first step toward falling headlong into it.

Such a humble awareness of temptation so gripped the apostle Paul that at the end of his ministry he no longer called himself an *apostle*. Instead he said, "Christ Jesus came into the world to save sinners; *of whom I am chief*" (1 Tim. 1:15, emphasis added). He recognized that anyone could sin.

Paul wrote, "Brethren, when someone errs, those who are spiritual, restore him in humility, lest you fall also" (Gal. 6:1, author's paraphrase). He referred to Christians falling for sin. I learned from Pastor LaFayette Scales that if we are truly spiritual, we must in humility acknowledge that we could do the same, then reach out a hand to help restore the fallen brother.

WARNING SIGNS OF DECEPTION

AFTER SEEING THE INSIDES OF MINISTRIES FAR-FLUNG ACROSS THE GLOBE, READING all the reports in my current ministry position and seeing the wreckage of people's lives, I have come up with some warning signs of deception that may be helpful.

1. *Different style of music*—When someone switches the radio from praise and worship to thug rap, something might be going on inside.

2. *Will not address or confront issues*—Some ministers do not want to confront people who are major contributors to their ministries, just as some businessmen do not want to confront good clients. Confidence in money can displace our belief that God is our source. Sometimes we just shy away from confronting because we are guilty of the same thing.

3. *Change in style of dress*—Not just a new change of clothes, but changing from conservative dress to clothes generally seen in a nightclub might mean something is wrong.

4. *New friendships and questionable associations*— Even those who clothe themselves with "godly" accoutrements can be bad friends.

5. *Change of sexual appetites*—We are fighting a plague today of pornography, which has found new fuel from the Internet. The conflagration is destroying lives from coast to coast. If you see suspicious websites on your computer's Internet memory, or awake in the night to find your spouse on the computer, fast and pray, go to your pastor or take your spouse to counseling!

6. *Preoccupation with things*—Consumed with self, excluding family or loyal friends and lavishing oneself with whatever can be acquired is a problem.

7. *A feeling of being the exception*—When confronted, the person may feel he or she does not need to

follow godly or moral guidelines. In the way some government officials feel they are above the law, some ministers can feel they are actually above the Word of God. I have heard ministers argue that they can live in sin and still be a Christian leader. That is deception.

8. *Increased or obvious pride in self or one's achievements*—When we think we are "somebody," we deceive, delude and cheat ourselves.

For if any person thinks himself to be somebody [too important to condescend to shoulder another's load] when he is nobody [of superiority except in his own estimation], he deceives and deludes and cheats himself. But let every person carefully scrutinize and examine and test his own conduct and his own work. He can then have the personal satisfaction and joy of doing something commendable.

—Galatians 6:3–4, AMP

---

1. This section on Solomon has been adapted from Charles R. Swindoll, *Insight for Living*, Bible Study Guide (n.p., n.d.), s.v. Solomon.

CHAPTER 6

THINGS THAT ATTRACT

I RESPECT PEOPLE LIKE MOTHER THERESA, WHO TRULY MADE A VOW OF poverty. But that is not to say I disrespect those who do not. I certainly believe in enjoying God's blessings.

I loved having more than enough. I enjoyed giving whatever I felt moved to give. I have not and would not do anything illegal to gain financial prosperity, but I enjoyed having it. Yet as Solomon discovered, financial prosperity can foster boredom. After all, only one outfit can be worn at a time. I once tried to fill the void in my heart with good works and things. Others fill such a void with food, sex, sports, hobbies and gossip.

Christians can become bored with God fairly easily. We know that is what is happening when we begin to say things like, "I've already studied that part of God's Word." "I've been to hear so-and-so, and I don't want to go again." "I'm getting a new translation of the Bible because I'm tired of the old one." "Is it Sunday? Let's skip church and go to breakfast!" We can become so familiar and blasé about God that we become complacent in the way we live our lives before Him.

Sometimes we need to give ourselves a little shake! And

sometimes God just shines His flashlight on us to show us the truth.

The last message I ever taught at Word of Faith Family Church was in the summer of 1992, on the subject of "landmarks." At that time, I had no idea I would never speak there again, but I am happy to remember my last topic. My husband and I had taken a break from the busyness brought on by the *PrimeTime Live* telecast. We were walking down the street in another city, window-shopping and sightseeing, and he was talking about his dreams of creating a side business and buying a new house in Florida. I remember suddenly throwing up my hands.

"I cannot do this anymore," I said as I spun around to face him. "I don't need another business or another house. I'm in the middle of all that I can handle right now."

At that instant, a flash from God of divine revelation made me realize that all the landmarks of our lives had been moved. At one time our boundaries had been purity and the honor of God. Now we were surrounded on all sides by "things" that caused trouble.

I was to teach that following Wednesday night. That evening I carefully chose my wardrobe, wearing things I owned that represented my very best. The congregation of fifteen hundred people was a good midweek crowd. I taught from Solomon's own proverb, "Remove not the ancient landmark" (Prov. 22:28). God sets boundaries for us that are our landmarks. He says to our hearts, "Don't do this" or "Do that." But our hearts become polluted as we allow those boundaries to be moved. Without God's boundaries firmly in place, the enemy comes and sows weeds we may not see immediately, but which will reap a bitter crop.

Jesus told the story of a farmer who planted good seed in his land. But as everyone slept, an enemy came and planted other seeds. The farmer had not posted a guard in the dark night hours, so his boundaries were invaded by the enemy without his knowledge. When the crop began to grow, tares grew among the wheat. "An enemy has done it!" the farmer realized. But all he could do was to allow the tares and wheat to grow together until the harvest. Then he had to sort the wheat from the tares, burning the useless tares. (See Matthew 13:24–32.)

The enemy longs to sow tares, or weeds, in the land of our hearts. He gets in through the eye gate or the ear gate, or by convincing us to move boundaries and landmarks, or by sneaking in during the darkness of trouble, depression or struggle to sow his despicable seeds. When we harvest a mixed crop, we need to get rid of the tares and burn them. We do not want those seeds coming up again.

That Wednesday night as I spoke, I told the congregation the lesson Solomon had learned—without God, everything else was meaningless. Then I took off my good shoes, found a woman who wore my size and gave them to her. I took off my good earrings and gave them to someone else. I took off my watch and gave it to another woman. I took off my necklace and gave it to a different lady. Everything I could take off and still remain decent, I gave away. I even promised my dress to someone else before I closed the service.

Sometimes we just have to signal to God that we are ready to restore the landmarks of our lives. We may have moved the landmarks over the years since we first began a business, got married, started a family or became a Christian. God will honor us when we honor Him by restoring the boundaries of our lives to where they were before compromise, confusion, deception or idolatry moved in.

MIXED CROPS

I GREW UP IN THE FARM COUNTRY SURROUNDING DAINGERFIELD, TEXAS. WE HAD miles and miles of fences that set the boundaries of those farms, sometimes bearing signs proclaiming, "Keep Out, No Trespassing." You and I need "No Trespassing" signs on our fences so the devil is afraid to enter with all his garbage! We need to send a message to every bearer of his bad seeds, "Keep off my land."

The seeds sown in our hearts have the power to attract or repel other elements. I have some plants around my back porch that attract bees. I do not want bees, so I need to pull up those plants. In the same way, if we do not want to get stung by what we are attracting, we have to clean out our hearts.

Perfect soil, however, does not exist. Stones, which represent our own flesh, always have to be plowed up. God reveals stones to us so we can pluck them up and throw them out of our land. His good seeds cannot take hold if they are competing with stones for the soil.

Christians accommodate fleshly "stones" and open their hearts to weeds, thinking they can get away with it, that it will not really matter. They may not even view sin as sin any longer, but simply as one of many "options." Such an attitude will certainly bring a "mixed crop" and possible disaster.

As our close friendships changed, a "mixed crop" began to grow up in our lives. In the wee hours of one 1987 morning, my husband suddenly sat straight up in bed, panic-stricken, panting as though he had been running. He said the devil had just come into our room to try to kill him, and the only way he had been able to wake up was by speaking the Word. He later wrote a book on the experience and preached it in church. He told me the devil's "imps" had not been able to do the job, so now Satan himself had come to kill him.

It was not long after this incident that I pointed out to him that what was going to kill him was the company he was keeping. The men who had ingratiated themselves with him seemed to have a stronger and stronger hold on his life. They became more important to him than family, church, ministry or even God. These were men with problems.

"Satan sent those men to kill you," I told him on several occasions. "They are demons from the pit of hell." Each time he became infuriated by my words and quickly jumped to their defense.

DECEPTION LEADS TO IDOLATRY

BEFORE OUR LIVES UNRAVELED, I WAS HAPPY WITH WHAT MY HUSBAND AND I were accomplishing, with the church and ministry we were building. To me, my husband also seemed completely fulfilled with the life we had created. But as I look back on it, I think as I became happier, he became less so. I believe we were both frustrated with at least some parts of our lives. At the least, prosperity did not bring as much happiness as you would think, and it often came with its own huge price tag.

My husband had always loved building houses, which he had done when we were first married. In 1988 he found a beautiful home in California for a price he insisted was too good to pass up. He started remodeling it, flying frequently to California. His instincts about the value of that house proved true. When the church sold it in February 1992, they netted a huge profit, almost doubling the investment. But that home was enormous, and it looked even bigger from the air.

As we launched into the lawsuits that followed the 1991 *PrimeTime Live* broadcast, my stomach would knot each evening when it was time for the news. Again and again I saw aerial views of that house in California, and the others we owned or rented at the time, splashed across the news. When the *PrimeTime Live* story broke, we had four homes. Although we were no longer living in the California home, it had not yet sold. When we moved back to Texas, the church rented us a home in Dallas while remodeling a different home for our permanent residence. That made three homes. Then, we had purchased a vacation home on a canal in Florida. That's the one my ex-husband lived in after the divorce and sold later for a song. Night after night pictures of those homes were flashed on television.

Then the media started on the boats. We had bought a boat in California, sold it and found a cabin cruiser in Florida. The media not only made the houses and boats an issue, but many of the nice things we could now afford became material for media attacks. The fact that no longer were we confined to what we could find at a discount department store caused great interest.

From the beginning of our ministry, we had believed the promise of God that if we gave up everything for the call of God on our lives, God would return it to us a hundredfold. God had indeed begun to fulfill that promise in our lives. But when prosperity came, along with it came temptations we had never experienced before and what seemed like justifiable reasons to give in to the temptations. With anything in life, physical or spiritual—until you go there, you do not know what you will find.

While most of us would never build a "golden calf" as the Israelites did, we are all susceptible to yielding to the temptation to build that idol slowly, just a minor increment every day.

Prosperity Is Tougher Than Adversity

SOLOMON WAS IMPECCABLE AT THE START OF HIS REIGN, HAVING THE BLESSING OF God, wealth, honor, insight, wisdom and broad interests. He was an architect, artist, entrepreneur and horticultural expert. But once he reached the top and had the esteem of the entire world, he became bored. When I read about Solomon, his life does not seem far different from the life of many of us today.

Thomas Carlisle stated, "Adversity is hard on a man, but for one man who can stand prosperity, there are a hundred that will stand adversity." Financial prosperity is one of the most difficult blessings to receive and one of the most difficult tests of character because of the temptations that come with it.

73

When you are deceived already, it is easy for prosperity to bring on idolatry, placing things above God. We easily make "gods" of things or people around us, and without even realizing it, we can start to enjoy pleasing them more than we enjoy pleasing God.

God told the Israelites not to touch the spoils of Jericho when it was defeated. But one man, Achan, saw a beautiful imported Babylonian robe, some coins and a gold bar, perhaps more beautiful than anything he had ever seen, and he took them. (See Joshua 7:20–26.) The command of God may have sounded easy until he saw what beauty and wealth existed, and then the tempter's voice overwhelmed his judgment. As a result, the entire army lost its next major battle, costing the lives of God's soldiers. All Achan could answer when Joshua interrogated him was that he saw it, he wanted it and he took it. He was killed for his sin—along with his entire household.

A popular expression asserts, "New levels, new devils." At each new level, we are exposed to new temptations, perhaps gift-wrapped with good works or disguised as a tremendous opportunity that seemingly could not hurt anyone. That is exactly what Adam and Eve fell for, and we all still feel the pain of their decision.

David was never as wise or as wealthy as his son Solomon. No one had charted that territory before. Whatever Solomon saw, if he wanted it, he took it. Wine, food and pleasure soon rivaled wisdom as Solomon's primary quest in life. He lived extravagantly (Eccles. 2:9–11). He built huge homes for himself and planted gardens and parks, with ingenious irrigation systems. He accumulated slaves, herds, storehouses of money, wives and concubines, and he sought ever more mental stimulation. Solomon had more money and wives than anyone ever had, yet he cheated other kings in business transactions and added an extra three hundred concubines to his harems. This is the nature of the flesh. What we have is never enough.

When nothing satisfied him any longer, Solomon did not know what to do with the emptiness. He said, "What do people get for all their hard work? Generations come and go, but nothing really changes. No matter how much we see, we are never satisfied. History merely repeats itself. Nothing under the sun is really new." (See Ecclesiastes 1.)

Toward the end of his life, Solomon recognized there was no peace, wisdom or joy apart from pleasing God. He advises us, "It's wonderful to be young.... But remember that you must give an account to God for everything you do.... Honor him in your youth before you grow old.... It will be too late then to remember him.... Fear God and obey his commands, for this is the duty of every person" (Eccles. 11:9; 12:1–2, 13–14, NLT). We can enjoy life, but we must give an account. Age works against us, because the longer we live without making God our priority, the fewer days we have.

The good things of life could not fulfill Solomon. "Things" also took their toll on my husband and me. Things started manipulating us. Once we started going along with them, things took us straight out of God's will. Jesus said this world's "things" can choke out the Word of God (Mark 4:19). Things can kill!

Often people confuse a perverse desire for things with prosperity. But Solomon's example is not my idea of living a prosperous life. To me, prosperity means mental, emotional, spiritual and physical health and well-being, as well as financially having enough, with plenty left over to help others. I believe this is God's blessing for His children. The Bible expository by W. E. Vine defines the common word blessing as "to cause to prosper, to make happy, to bestow blessings on."

I am sure the people of his day discussed their views on Solomon. Some probably looked at the end of his life and renounced his teaching. But Solomon's proverbs were incorporated into our Holy Bible, the standard of our lives. There was nothing wrong with Solomon's philosophies and proverbs, but everything wrong with the way he lived his life after he compromised his walk with God.

People have asked if I still believe God wants to prosper us. I absolutely believe in the Word of God. I believe every scripture from Genesis to Revelation. I believe Psalm 1, that I am like a tree planted by the rivers of water, that I will bring forth fruit in my season, that none of my leaves will die but all will flourish and that everything I set my hand to will prosper. I believe my God will supply every one of my needs according to His riches in glory by Christ Jesus. I can thank my Father that Jesus Himself bore infirmities in His own body on the tree. My children and I, being dead to sin, live unto righteousness, and by His stripes we were healed.

This is a far cry from believing we should buy whatever we can afford—and even things we cannot afford—with no restraint. The lust for things and deceitfulness of riches is a pitfall. God said it—*the love of money* corrupts! (See 1 Timothy 6:10.) I believe the adage, "It is not wrong to have money, but it is wrong for money to have you." I am personally worn out from seeing people judge others' spirituality based on their financial prosperity.

Eye Gates and Ear Gates

The Bible says, "Out of the same mouth proceedeth blessing and cursing" (James 3:10). From the same field grow good crops and weeds.

Jesus said, "Blessed are your eyes, for they see: and your ears, for they hear" (Matt. 13:16). The eyes and ears are the gates to our land through which the enemy can sow weeds. Starting with those in leadership over us or role models whom we follow, and continuing with those with whom we associate, we can open ourselves to all kinds of goodness—or to all kinds of wickedness. We can easily accept a lifestyle we normally would not accept just because we like the person who intro-duces it to us.

Jesus said if we "even look"—meaning sowing an image in our hearts and meditating on it—we commit that sin. (See Matthew 5:28.) The next time we have the opportunity, we might look twice. When we are conditioned and ripe, the devil sends along a "sweet fruit" attractive enough to fall for. Watching pornography on the Internet is a seed sown. At first we want to turn it off, but when that seed germinates, the next time a naked person pops up on our screen, we might not be so fast to hit "delete"! Or perhaps we open our ear gate to listen to an off-color joke. Even the strongest, most holy and wise Christian can fall if the heart is not guarded. This is what happened with Solomon.

Divorce is a great example. Some people make commitments never to divorce. But the more they are surrounded with people who have been divorced, or have poor marriages, or are adul-terous, seeds are sown of the "possibility" of divorce. I am a divorced woman today, but I believe God's Word, which says, "For the LORD God of Israel says that He hates divorce" (Mal. 2:16, NKJV). I recognize as much as anyone that divorce is not always avoidable. Yet I am grieved, especially when Christian leaders divorce, stay out of the public eye for a year or so, then return right back to their position in leadership, depending upon people to forget and unconditionally accept their new lives, or new spouses, as if nothing had ever happened.

As go the leaders, so go the people. The apostle Paul said, "Who did hinder you that ye should not obey the truth?...A little leaven leaveneth the whole lump...but he that troubleth you shall bear his judgment, whosoever he be" (Gal. 5:7, 9–10). Our faith gets unsettled when we are motivated by selfishness. Only a "little leaven" is needed to send us off course. I have heard that in the space program, rockets are on target only 3 percent of the time; the rest of the time is spent making course corrections.

> Hearing you will hear and shall not understand, and seeing you will see and not perceive; for the hearts of this people have grown dull. Their ears are hard of hearing, and their eyes they have closed, lest they should see with their eyes and hear with their ears, lest they should understand with their hearts and turn, so that I should heal them.
>
> —MATTHEW 13:14–15, NKJV

Even though we open our ear gate and eye gate to God, we cannot turn to Him when our hearts are hard. Jesus said Moses allowed divorce because of the hardness of heart, "but from the beginning it was not so" (Matt. 19:8). Jesus also said, "What therefore God hath joined together, let not man put asunder" (Matt. 19:6).

I received a call from the wife of one of my husband's friends after my divorce was announced. "Your marriage was never meant to be," she said.

My response was, "Well, tell God that, and tell my four children." This kind of thinking shows a hardhearted mentality. What about the vow we made before God and to each other? I am not saying abused spouses must stay in abusive marriages. But we need a measure of the fear of God. God says, "I hate divorce."

RESTORING THE SOUL

OFTEN WE PRAY AND ARE DELIVERED OF VARIOUS SPIRITUAL, INNER BONDAGES IN our lives, yet we almost always need to take corresponding actions in the physical realm to see the deliverance completed. Like the entrapment of sin, deliverance rarely is completed overnight. We can complain when God does not take care of it for us all at once, but God is a master at building fine humans fit for His work. He knows how to bring us through tests of our faith in order to refine us and ensure that we do not travel that pathway again.

When I was first born again, I smoked three packs of cigarettes a day. At age twenty-two, I could not even walk two blocks without gasping for breath. Today, I work out for over an hour most nights and feel terrific. Although I wanted to stop smoking for my health, only when I started reading the Word every day did I see those cigarettes as bondage. Even though I prayed for deliverance and went to altar services to be delivered, I was only delivered by faith. I still had the craving for cigarettes in the natural realm.

I would throw my cigarettes away, then start craving them again. My husband had our only car, so I would put Amy in a stroller and walk many city blocks to a store for cigarettes. I could hardly wait to get back home to smoke. But as soon as I lit up, I would be mad, realizing I was allowing those things to overpower me and keep me from deliverance. I would be so disgusted that I would put the cigarette out, tear up the rest and flush them down the toilet. Then a few hours later, Amy would go back in her stroller, and I would start walking again. Over a period of three months, I went through this routine countless times, but never finished one cigarette. Then one day the craving was gone. The deliverance had already taken effect in the spirit realm, but I was not delivered in the physical realm until I had corresponding actions.

Moses had to keep going back to Pharaoh again and again to get deliverance for his people. God had already promised deliverance and had provided it in the spirit realm, but the bondage only grew worse at first. Moses had to persevere in the physical realm, asking Pharaoh ten times, before the deliverance God intended came.

We cannot become so discouraged as we restore our boundaries and kick things out of our hearts that we simply give in and let the stones and weeds choke us. It may take some doing, but we can be free. "If the Son therefore shall make you free, ye shall be free indeed" (John 8:36)!

FEAR THE LORD!

...AL PEOPLE HAVE TOLD ME THEY NEVER FORGOT THE MESSAGE I TAUGHT ON "landmarks." Someone even had the tape and gave me a copy of it later. I will never forget the light God shone on that day when I started moving landmarks back into place in my own life.

Cleaning our hearts, putting away idolatry—meaning anything that has crept into our lives that rivals our devotion to God—and serving the Lord always starts with the fear of the Lord. The following scriptures help us to understand the importance of fearing God:

> Now therefore fear the LORD, and serve him in sincerity and in truth: and put away the gods which your fathers served...and serve ye the LORD.
>
> —JOSHUA 24:14

> The fear of the LORD is the beginning of knowledge: but fools despise wisdom and instruction.
>
> —PROVERBS 1:7

> If you will revere and fear the Lord and serve Him and hearken to His voice and not rebel against His commandment, and if both you and your king will follow the Lord your God, it will be good!
>
> —1 SAMUEL 12:14, AMP

> What man is he that feareth the LORD? him shall he teach in the way that he shall choose.
>
> —PSALM 25:12

> Oh how great is thy goodness, which thou hast laid up for them that fear thee.
>
> —PSALM 31:19

When the opportunity arises, why would we not allow God to deal with our hearts? Why would we not repent? What could possibly hold us back? Shame? Pride? Nothing is worth more, or gives more, than cleaning ourselves before God.

Jesus came in the likeness of flesh, in a body that holds sin, yet He was without taint of sin. Having lived a sinless life, He died under judgment for our sin, our lawlessness, our missing the mark. Today He gives us boundaries to live within for our own peace of mind and prosperity of spirit.

If I can be delivered from all that encroached on my land, certainly you can be free, too. Be quick to restore the landmarks of your life. Maybe it is time to create new boundaries formed out of the convictions of your heart. Every day that you continue living outside the landmarks and boundaries God has ordained for you is a day lost to God's purposes for your life.

CHAPTER 7

TIME TO TAKE
RESPONSIBILITY

W E TEND TO THINK WE KNOW OURSELVES BETTER THAN WE ACTUALLY
do. We see others in their grief, trials or troubles
and think, *If that were me, I'd…* But we generally do
not know what we would do under those circumstances until
we are in them, complete with all the torrents of emotion that
cloud our judgment. Seeing how we respond in such situations can be a shocking revelation. But even finding out what
is in our hearts will not help unless we are willing to accept
responsibility for it.

Compromise causes confusion. "If a godly man compromises with the wicked, it is like polluting a fountain or mud-
dying a spring" (Prov. 25:26, TLB). We have streams in East Texas
with thick silt bottoms. If you put a stick in one and stir just a
little, it will muddy the entire stream, at least for a time. My
entire self-image had been temporarily polluted, and my relationship with God was muddied. I kept trying to be better
based on what others said, trying to become a person I was
never going to become. I had built a little world in my mind in
which my husband loved me and was proud of me, and I was

helping him as he flew around the world getting people saved. I thought it was reality.

Little hints appeared, but in the confusion I could not see them clearly enough to let them concern me. Instead, unless something was flagrantly wrong, I went blindly along with whatever came up. I remember when my husband announced to the congregation that we were leaving for California. He did not mention the illness that was leading him to make the move, but instead he said that he had had a dream about going down a road that led past the church. He said it meant that he was going to be the "apostle" of the church, but not the resident pastor. He told the church he was going to start an international office in California.

His decision to move to California was a unilateral one, but because it was based on doctors' recommendations, I went along with it. However, I felt confused and hurt that he didn't tell the congregations the "real" reason he was leaving, which was the illness.

Later, when we started legal procedures that dealt with our first amendment rights, I went along with the flow of the legal reasoning of those around me. I had always believed that the Bible called us to walk a straight and narrow path. But now when I heard a doctrine with which I disagreed, people told me, "Marte, they have the right to believe that. Just because you don't believe it doesn't mean it's wrong." Already pressured and confused, I quieted down and wondered if I were indeed a judgmental person who had no right to open my mouth in defense of my beliefs in God. In the battle for the right to free speech, I lost mine.

I Am Not God!

Although I knew practically everything about the day-to-day operations of the church, I was totally in the dark about the things my husband was doing with his friends and the plans that he and the lawyer were making. We were living two different lives, and I cannot take responsibility for his life. But I accept responsibility for what I know was in my own heart. I got caught up in pride with what I was doing for God's kingdom. I had grown to depend upon my own strength. Instead of chasing what God had for me, I started chasing the image of "Superwoman," which was completely unattainable. But that does not mean I am guilty for the actions of others. Even though I do not blame others, that does not mean I accept their guilt. I can only accept responsibility for what is truly mine.

I have learned that taking responsibility from someone else is like any other form of stealing—it robs an important part of that person's life. That person needs to accept responsibility for his or her own life. This was another blind spot for me. I accepted the blame and responsibility for everything that went wrong in the marriage. At the time of the divorce, I believed something in me was so wrong that it could never be corrected.

After the *PrimeTime Live* telecast, we hired professional investigators who combed through our staff for leaks. They surfaced an employee who they believed had "leaked" information to the media. I was blamed for pointing him out—too late to prevent the leak—and told never to return to my office. I was ordered out of church operations by my husband. My salary was cut to a third, and I was told I could work only at the school. A relative of the woman who would become my husband's second wife became the administrator, although I was told by others that the church lawyer virtually made the decisions. Yet to my knowledge, no discipline was ever given to the person who was the "leak."

Confused, I wondered if I was so bad that even God had no use for me. I thought that because I did not buy into my husband's new vision for our future and ministry, and since he was the "man of God" and people were still being saved and healed, because God was not stopping what was happening, the problem must be mine. It was a very confusing mind game. This was in stark contrast to how I had seen myself earlier.

Only a proud heart would believe it could fix everything! On the surface, the "fixer" appears to be humbly sacrificing to serve others, yet "fixing" can stem from pride and end in disaster for those the "fixer" is trying to serve. The term *enabling* is used by psychologists to describe this attempt to fix things for others.

For years my typical day consisted of waking at four, praying and reading the Word, exercising, dressing, waking the children, making breakfast for the family, serving my husband's breakfast on a tray, whisking the kids off to school, then going to work. In the afternoons, I left the office, picked up the children, checked the homework—with Marcus pounding the breakfast bar as he screamed, "I don't like my A-B-Cs"—while I made a light dinner with farm-raised meats and vegetables. Matt would always bend over his dinner plate, sniff and say, "What dat 'mell?" After dinner, I would get the kids off to bed, then relax with my husband, if he was home, before retiring for the night.

I was trying to help everyone and keep the lids on everything that was boiling over. "Fixing" can easily become competition with God Himself. I had become a little "god" without even realizing it. For a time, I thought myself to be so capable! Once our finances were back on track and our savings accounts were growing, the final trap sprang, and I no longer recognized my need to find my sufficiency in the Lord Jesus Christ. I was a self-sufficient woman. Everything we were doing was working. Our telephone center was popping with calls. People were being saved and healed. People's finances were being increased. Departments within the ministry were working with each other well. Every system I devised with which to operate the ministry was oiled to perfection, and we were operating at what I thought was maximum efficiency. I would probably have volunteered to run the world if God needed help!

But instead of loving me for "helping" them, people resented me and started finding fault with almost everything I did. Some told me I was too fat for television, and I almost became anorexic trying to lose weight and exercise. I even gave up chips, which for me is like giving up air! One day a secretary told me my husband wanted a *wife*, not an *administrator.* I just looked at her and wondered why a secretary was telling me that! Others on staff called me "Jezebel." A Jezebel is an enabler, but with an evil purpose. I thought I was trying to help for the right reasons, but I ended up accomplishing all the wrong things.

There is so much I could have done so differently. We could easily have hired a top-notch administrator. I could have delegated responsibility, pressed further into the Word of God and prayer, gone for codependent counseling and made probably thousands of other changes. I had options. But in the confusion, I lived as though I had none.

I used to think, *God has really given me a lot of strength, because I never would have thought that I could do all this.* Being a naturally industrious person, I certainly would not have gone the other way—become a slacker—for the world. My husband and I were from hardworking stock that took pride in making do rather than giving up. When we could not support ourselves in ministry while driving around the country in that trailer, we planted our kids in the car and parked it next to jobs where we built fences together to pay our way. I unloaded the slats. He hammered them.

I later prided myself that I was willing to do so much. I would have killed myself trying to do it all. Stopping me may have been an act of God's mercy to bring me back on track with Him. God wanted me in the place where He was my sufficiency and my source, not myself. How I was stopped was not something God necessarily caused. I think that what I did, I did to myself.

Even when I saw our foundations cracking, instead of leaning on the Lord for wisdom, I continued "doing." A few years later when I knew my husband was contemplating divorce, I prayed, "Lord, please change his mind. Help me." But God told my heart distinctly that my husband would never accept responsibility for his actions until I stopped covering for him so he could become accountable to God once again.

Give It a Rest!

I WAS ALWAYS TRYING TO HOLD IT TOGETHER, GET IT ON THE RIGHT TRACK—FIX IT! When guest ministers who came to our church to speak would ramble on for hours, not respecting people's time, I would think, *When will he get on with it? Mercy! In order to be super-woman, I have to get up at 4:00. Let me get home, bathe my babies and get to bed!*

There was always another event to prepare for, artwork to approve and other "stuff" to accomplish. Those were telltale signs that the ministry drove us instead of us driving the ministry, but I did not discern it. I had things I "had" to do—document miracles to use on the next television program, write manuals to comply with the law, establish policies and procedures for every new project, oversee the departments to keep them working as a team instead of intentionally delaying work because of personality clashes, check with the bookkeeper for balances and whether the mail was delivered promptly to the bank, check with data processing to ensure they received and processed the mail and prayer requests—and on and on it went.

Anything can become your master. Say you buy a silver coffee set for your home. First you need to polish it to protect your investment, so you may carve out time to do that yourself or hire someone. Next you install a home security system so no one can steal it. Then you buy or increase your insurance policy so it is covered. Then you want to take a vacation, but you have to have someone house-sit to ensure that you are not robbed. Soon all this activity surrounds one measly purchase. We do the same with cars, jewelry, dogs, RVs—you name it!

Television worked the same way. First you have an available building, so you think, *Why rent a studio and waste all that money when we can tape our programs right here?* So you install walls that block out the sound. You shop for equipment, which consultants have to figure out for you, and you hire experts to install it. The experts say the consultants purchased the wrong thing. When you finally hire a crew to use the equipment, they hand in purchase orders to get another brand. You need a water-cooled air conditioning system to ensure you keep the equipment running, the electric bill for which can easily be six thousand dollars a month in a hot state like Texas. Then you need security guards to monitor the building because of all the money you have invested.

Finally you are ready to do the television taping. Lights! Action! But that program cannot air without an opening introduction and a closing. You could edit the tapes somewhere else, but because you are going to be producing long term and have already built a whole studio, it seems cheaper to install an editing suite in your building. Who knows, someone may rent it from you sometime so you can actually make some money on it. Pretty soon you have a big building, and a big mess that is not only running you, but is continually demanding more.

By 1988 the church was no longer growing, and I wondered why. The television ministry was increasing, though, so my husband appeared to resent the church because it seemed like a drain. I remember people at the school saying, "We need this" or "that," and I would say, "Well, the school can't afford that because the television ministry is really supporting the school right now."

When my husband complained that he was tired of asking for the "vow" on his television program, I told him to take a sabbatical and ask God what he should be doing. But we had eight hundred people on staff, and he said that he could not take time off because he had to provide for all of them. He would not even consider downsizing.

Sometimes we need to step back from our endeavors, take a fresh look and gain heaven's perspective about all we are doing. Our "land" must be given a rest. *Sabbath* is not just an Old Testament law, but a truth for us all. After being thrown out of the office and the church buildings, I think I had to make up for the Sabbaths I had not previously taken. When Israel refused to rest the land God had given them, He sent them into exile for a period of time equal to the amount of time they robbed the land.

We must take time for a Sabbath, to get before God, seek Him and become restored. A minister's Sabbath cannot be Sunday, so there must be another day, or days, when we take off, completely away from the ministry. It is hard to do because people are always going to have needs. But the one who most needs us to keep busy is Satan. That is how he can trap us. Satan is like a lion waiting for his prey to be off guard. He is ready to spring at the first opportunity.

I remember now how our mentor, John Osteen, refused to become stressed over anything. He meditated on the Word at home, and he would not even return calls unless he wanted to! That is the way I remember him. He was a smart man and took care of business. He died an honorable man because he watched out for his spirit-life and did not let the ministry run him.

FEAR PREVENTS RESPONSIBILITY

FEAR DID SOMETHING ELSE TO ME. IN THE MIDEIGHTIES WHEN I REALIZED WE had made mistakes in setting up the accounting procedures for the church, we hired a lawyer who was recommended to my husband by another minister. He seemed absolutely gleeful to discover I was willing to do whatever he said in order to create a "perfect" nonprofit corporation. Our annual church operation was growing, eventually reaching an income of roughly seventy million dollars annually. We felt it was prudent to have outside help.

We instituted severe accounting procedures whereby my husband and I could never actually touch any of the church's money, other than our salaries, which were based on the midrange in surveys of other nonprofit corporations the same size.

We had been so careful because lawyers had always told us that the Internal Revenue Service would investigate us. A giant bogeyman existed in the government, and it was out to get every ministry. The attorney said, "It is not a matter of *if* but *when*." Actually, the attorney general's office was painted the same way, which resulted in my biggest mistake ever.

Our attitude toward the IRS may have given the impression that we had something to hide. High-level IRS agents flew in after the *PrimeTime Live* report and sat with us around a lawyer's boardroom table to start an audit, both for the church and for us personally, that would last for three years. There I sat in my navy blue suit, fully confident inside that they would find nothing. Nothing is exactly what they found during three tedious years—nothing. The agents agreed with our salaries, commended me for good documentation and were some of the most respectful people I met during that period of my life.

I realize now that my fears of this government adversary had been misplaced. Some rude agents may have harassed, intimidated and hurt American citizens. But that was not my experience. Ironically, I had more reason to fear my own lawyers who had a fiduciary duty to act in my best interest. But I did not know that until later.

My misplaced trust became useful to those around me who wanted to control and manipulate my actions. Had I stepped off the racetrack long enough, I may have avoided some of the consequences through which I am still living. Looking back, some fears are similar to a child's believing a bogeyman is under the bed, and just as groundless. We need to listen to God speak to our hearts and heed Him when He tells us, "Fear not." We need Him to switch on the lights in the darkness of our soul and show us our fears are nothing more than shadows, which can do us no harm.

The fear of man was one of the tools Satan used to take down Saul's kingdom when he was Israel's king. God commanded him to wipe out the Amalekites and to destroy all their possessions in order to settle His account for their sins against Israel. God does settle His accounts! Saul went to battle, but he would not destroy the best things because, as he explained to Samuel, the people demanded to have them, and he feared the people. Fear of man! And lust for things.

Instead of repenting, Saul argued, "But I *did* obey the Lord." God immediately lifted His hand from Saul and rejected him as king. Even when Saul finally repented, he could not win back his crown. Samuel looked for Saul's replacement in the house of Jesse. David was not the tallest or the most handsome, but God said He did not look at outward appearances. He looked at the heart. Still today, God is looking at our hearts, not at what we do.

When Saul saw David after he was chosen, Saul saw the anointing that had once been his own. Saul forfeited the Spirit of God. In place of the anointing, he was given a tormenting spirit of depression and fear. God is not tolerant of disobedience!

Disobedience and fear can lead to an inability to be responsible for your own actions. They can also cause one to feel responsible for another's actions. Today I have learned to take responsibility for my own actions—and reactions. And I have learned that I am not responsible for the mistakes others make.

However, I shall always regret the effects that the actions of all of the people involved in the events of the past decade or more have had on innocent bystanders such as the wonderful people of our church and on the lives of my own children. In the next chapter we will take a close look at how these events have affected the lives of my children.

CHAPTER 8

INNOCENT VICTIMS
—MY CHILDREN

T HE INNOCENT VICTIMS OF ANY CRISIS, SETBACK OR DISASTER ARE ALWAYS
the children. A dad loses his business, and wondering
why, the wide-eyed children move from their house into
an apartment. A mom refuses to subject herself to physical
abuse any longer, and the children's roots are ripped up as
they are taken to a shelter. A little brother contracts leukemia,
and the big brother's childhood is suspended as the family
rallies to help the sick child.

When the crisis is avoidable, the tragedy for the children is
even more pronounced. My two youngest children were
uprooted from the home they had lived in for many years, and
all four of my children were prevented from entering the only
church they had known.

People who create the crises for others often say they are not
hurting anyone. But they are deceived by believing that no one
else is hurt by their actions. The choices they make that are
based on their selfish will require those around them to live
through the consequences—right along with them. After
Achan stole the Babylonian robe, the Israelites went to battle at

Ai, a country easy to beat, but they lost. Achan's sin affected the entire nation. As a result, his entire family was stoned, then burned. (See Joshua 7.)

In the same way today, when one parent or spouse makes choices, the entire family either suffers or prospers—and often others as well. Today more than 50 percent of American homes are single-parent homes, generally led by a mother. Over twenty-six million children are fatherless. This certainly qualifies as a modern-day plague.

The cruel "god of Molech" is still alive today. (See Leviticus 20.) In the Old Testament, the Israelites started worshiping this foreign god that required the sacrifice of living children for the parents' selfish desires of success and prosperity. Still today, parents sacrifice their children for their own wealth or success. We have our own gods of cruelty. These gods include:

- Selfishness—"I want my own way."
- Stubbornness—"I won't quit until I get it."
- Indifference—"I don't care who it hurts."
- Resistance—"I refuse to listen to counsel."
- Contempt—"I'm not concerned about the consequences."

Christians tend to act horrified at the numbers of abortions, yet we are not in any way horrified when upstanding citizens sacrifice their children's well-being for the sake of their own desires or gain. We try to increase the family's bottom line, sometimes at the price of the kids. This is exactly what we did when my husband gave in to divorce rather than submit to counseling.

The solution is to serve the Lord only and put no gods, including our own desires, before Him. When we worship Him above all others, then our hearts are bent on obeying Him, pleasing Him and following His commands.

Regardless of the circumstances, we must learn to point our children toward God as well. The Word says the Holy Spirit is our teacher. I cannot "fix" or live my children's lives, but I can trust the Holy Spirit to take care of them. As I do my part, He does His part. I can help them through the rejection they have faced. I can assure them they are OK. I can help them to look at themselves the way God looks at them. And I can point them to God and His Word. Then the scripture is fulfilled that says, "All thy children shall be taught of the LORD; and great shall be the peace of thy children" (Isa. 54:13).

DINNER PARTIES

I LOVE ENTERTAINING. ONE OF OUR FORMER FAMILY TRADITIONS WAS THAT I SPENT most Saturdays preparing the Sunday meal for our family and whoever else was brought home. Generally a good number of friends would come over, and we would always have an enjoy-able—and very noisy—time. Even though we had china and crystal on the table, we were as loud as a room full of Italian cooks.

After the divorce, I kept the same routine, cooking on Saturdays, preparing the table, setting out the china and crystal, cutting fresh flowers or making an arrangement, color-coordinating the linens. This was fun to me. Toward the end of 1996, when I told the Lord I had to get out of the tunnel, I changed a few routines and realized family dinners had actu-ally become ruts. We started having them less frequently and without as many people. Now we tend to be more excited when we have dinner together. Sometimes the children and I are the only guests, but we still use the china and crystal, and we are still as loud as the floor of the stock exchange.

At one such dinner recently, we were all there except my oldest son, Jon, who lives out of state. Amy and her husband, Bill, came over with my grandchildren, Reagan and Makena, who love "Nana's house." They love their uncles who live with me too, my teenagers Marc and Matt. As we were gathered that night, I was mulling over my writing of this book. I asked my children what they thought about our home as it was before the divorce. One said our home had been happy, and that their father and I rarely argued. If we did, it was always over a staff problem or one of his friends.

We all reminisced about the different things we had done... the places where we had vacationed. We talked about our years as a family. We remembered how tough the media attacks had been—and their effects upon our family. We talked about the greater heartache of the disjointing of our family. And we praised God that we still have each other.

Looking back over the years, I realize now that my silence had helped subject my children to the snide remarks and cruel jokes from people who have never had the opportunity to have all the facts. I thought I was protecting my children, when in fact I had imprisoned us all in my closet of silence.

Hardly a week goes by without my children suffering some ill effect from their name. The week after that family dinner, I discovered that my oldest teen was told he would not receive a raise at work because his mother was "rich." He went to his manager, who evidently knew more about labor laws than the supervisor, and received his raise. I am certain none of my children have told me everything to which they have been subjected, although I do know a few things.

In talking with them about the past, I also realized that we once had a happy home. And it is happy today.

DREAM WORLDS

ABOUT A YEAR AGO, IN RESPONSE TO A FAX, I WROTE TO MY EX-HUSBAND TO TELL him I realized that although I thought I was married to a prince, when I opened my eyes, it was really a frog. When I needed him the most, he disappeared in the fog of my imagination. He had changed—he was not whom I imagined him to be. We had an animated conversation when he received the letter. I forgave him for not being the person I had created in my mind. He asked for my forgiveness in general—never for the specific way he had hurt me.

In the months and years following the divorce, I slowly faced the fact that I had created a fantasy. The world inside my head was not real. I was not, nor could I ever be, Superwoman. My ex-husband was no longer someone who had earned the trust I extended—trust I had clung to right through the divorce and for years following it. I had created an idealized image in my mind, and when the world was not the way I thought it should be, I tried to pretend it was, defending him in every deposition, court trial and lawsuit. The reality was a bitter pill.

Suddenly I had to deal with the fact that what my dad had always said was far too close to being right. As it turned out, it seemed that as a woman, I had been good only at making babies and keeping good records. My dad's belief that preachers were nothing but hot air that wanted money seemed to fit the situation. I had fought those stereotypes all my life, but his words tracked me down and threw me to the ground, wounding me deeply, trying to isolate me from my God-given destiny. If I succumbed to the cynical grip of those words, I could have lost the dignity of my femininity and the future the Lord had for me in ministry. Coming to grips with truth, while struggling against such lies and accusations of the devil, was an emotional and spiritual minefield.

Children in the home pick up the spirit that is in the home. They can sense even in the womb what is happening with their parents. My children were cute and nicely dressed throughout the years. But because of my own denial of the truth in the later years of my marriage, I put them in a position to live in my fantasy, telling them everything would work out and covering for their dad. At some point we had all been really happy. But my children had sensed, long before I allowed myself to know, that something was terribly wrong.

We all have within our nature the ability to create "dream worlds." Every girl dreams of her knight in shining armor. He comes riding in, kills the giants and picks her up with his strong arm, and they ride off into the sunset. Every guy dreams of being the knight in shining armor, rescuing the helpless girl and whisking her away. Then one day she finds out that he is human. He is not always that strong, he is often insecure, he cannot make a living for her the way she dreamed, and her disappointment can turn to anger or rebellion.

Likewise, he finds out that she is human. She can think for herself, has her own ideas, no longer thinks everything he says is brilliant and has expectations of him that he does not think he can fulfill. His disappointment can cause him to manipulate her, to try to press her into a shape she does not fit, because he cannot let go of the ideal in his mind.

For many years I was told I was "dumb," that I would become a victim of my own stupidity. But as reality burst upon my mind, I realized I was never dumb. I was trusting. I had been taught to trust in the Lord, to trust in my ex-husband and to stand behind him. When his behavior changed and his actions were suspicious at best, his friends had criticized me, saying I should continue supporting his every whim, regardless of what he did. My real problem was just the opposite, because I did exactly that for far too long.

I refused to violate my heart any more than I had already done, but I admit I wanted to continue to trust. Because I refused to open my eyes to what was happening, I allowed my children to become victims. I did not fight for their future, and I made decisions that gave up their financial security as well.

BAD ROLE MODELS

As frustrating as it is to share children with an estranged spouse, I know better than to fall for cynicism and hatred. People are drawn away and enticed by their own lusts. "When lust hath conceived, it bringeth forth sin: and sin, when it is finished, bringeth forth death" (James 1:15). *Certainly there is something better in life* is really just lustful thinking. When we start looking around because we are hurt in our situation, bored in our marriage or cynical in our church, Satan will always accommodate our lusts. When we meditate on how much we dislike an ex-spouse or employer, or how unfair others are, Satan will be sure to send us friends who agree, providing the support we need to fall for his traps. Then sin is conceived, which brings death. Whether it be lust, greed, self-centeredness, jealousy or a host of other negative emotions and desires, Satan knows how to take us to the edge, then give us the not-so-gentle tap to send us headlong into his pit.

The same devil worked in the same way on the perpetrators of whatever evil you are up against today. Perpetrators are so deceived that they believe any decision they want to make is OK—regardless of whom it affects. Satan helps them to justify it in their minds. To them, they are OK and everyone else is wrong. To them, everyone else is the cause of the destruction they themselves caused.

Yet often these people believe that God is pleased with them. They make rationalizing statements: "You have to love me to be a Christian." "I am trying to be a friend to your mother/father." "I'm only asking that you accept me for who I am." These are tricky statements that make the perpetrator sound reasonable and right. As a result, emotionally abused spouses end up supporting the unfaithful person. Physically abused spouses hope for the day the other will change.

In the church, people are often pushed in our faces to be accepted as godly when they are anything but. I do not understand how Christians can sweep a perpetrator's unbridled lusts under the carpet and continue to believe anything that comes out of that person's mouth. Yet it happens all the time. For example, the steel mill president's daughter deals drugs, and church folks look the other way because they want the president's offerings to continue. Or the soloist commits adultery, and because we think we need his talents, we choose to believe he was forced into it by a lousy wife.

In my case, I never really acknowledged how bad things were. Maybe I knew about certain things all along, or knew something was wrong, but I hid it even from myself. I stayed home with the children and the church while my ex-husband escaped to different parts of the country. I became the strong person he and the lawyers later accused me of being, not because I was naturally strong or even wanted to be, but because I felt our children and congregation needed stability and encouragement. Someone needed to be responsible. I did not know my husband was doing exactly what he had always taught—"Don't drop one plan until you have another."

It is time we all stop making excuses! Christians need to call sin "sin" again instead of calling it someone's "problem." And it is high time we stop extending grace at the expense of our children.

I sought various people's counsel during those latter years, all of whom told me to go along with what was happening. The more I heard that, the more isolated I felt, as if I was not allowed to express what was pressing down on me. I kept up the front, though, never seeing how it was affecting my children.

People did try to talk to my ex-husband, I believe to bring some correction and balance, but he tended to ignore those who did not agree with him. So they left. I wish they had told me their views, but I certainly am not one who can blame their silence. I will come back to this later.

REAL ROLES

I BELIEVED THAT CHILDREN WERE A MOTHER'S RESPONSIBILITY—OLD-FASHIONED thinking I picked up while growing up in my little East Texas town. Dutifully I became a mother for my children, administrator for the church, political activist, founder of a school for the congregation's children. I did not become anything for myself. Blinded by duty, I saw only a glimmer of what God had planted in my own heart.

Children are influenced by the parent who is with them the most. When they are little, a mother generally tries to make their day fun. Then they come to an age when fathers make sure that at least their boys are doing sports and their daughters are active as well. Mothers generally make sure their boys are well groomed and their girls have a wardrobe. But what impression are parents really giving them? Are we letting them know there is equal dignity and worth in both mother and father?

When one spouse tries to force the other into a particular image, the result is mind control, manipulation, nagging, blackmail, ultimatums and constant strife. As spouses, we can start thinking so low of ourselves that we believe the best job we can find is passing out fliers at the neighborhood discount department store—and never rise above that. And we pass this along to our children by our actions.

This is especially a trap for single mothers. Our children need to see us digging into our own hearts for what God has given us and believing God for our future. Our children need to see us reach some goals in life! God gives the ideas and inspiration to make it through life. He does not leave us helpless and alone, even though that is how we feel. We must renew our minds through reading and hearing the Word—particularly if we have been beaten down.

We cannot depend on a spouse doing what he or she is supposed to do. We cannot depend on a parent to do what he or she is supposed to do. We cannot depend on business partners, employees, the government always doing what they are supposed to do. We must become dependent on God, believing Him to do what He said He would do, and learning to make it on our own. God is our spouse and a Father to our children.

This is so difficult for single parents. Many women do not want to try to fill a man's role as head of the household. We want to be cared for, protected, encouraged and allowed to pursue our dreams as we raise our children. We want our children to be loved, nourished and provided for by their father so they can grow up with a good perspective of the Father God. But so often we have to step into that place because the man refuses to be a man—leaving us little choice. Likewise a single father feels the need to fulfill the mother's role, for which he may feel incredibly inept.

God created husband and wife to walk side by side. That is physically the only way we can walk. The "Proverbs 31 Woman" was the consummate wife, mother and business-woman. She arose spiritually in times of darkness. She arose materially, mentally, emotionally and physically as well, and she submitted herself to her husband. The husband's chief responsibility in Scripture is to love his wife "even as Christ also loved the church, and gave himself for it" (Eph. 5:25). The husband is to "provoke not your children to wrath: but bring them up in the nurture and admonition of the Lord" (Eph. 6:4).

The children's responsibility is to "obey your parents in the Lord: for this is right. Honour thy father and mother; which is the first commandment with promise; that it may be well with thee, and thou mayest live long on the earth" (Eph. 6:1–3). My oldest grandchild is learning those verses right now, and my children laugh as he recites them, remembering back to when they memorized them as well. The Scripture tells us the way life ought to be!

As I discussed our situation with my children, I finally real-ized that it was high time to clarify for their sakes the biblical order of life. They needed to know that when times are tough, a man does not put all the responsibility of business, home and children on his wife—while he is running away to create a new life.

WHAT CHILDREN NEED TO KNOW

SMALL CHILDREN PICK UP A LACK OF HARMONY IN THE HOME AT THE EARLIEST OF ages, but they cannot pinpoint the actual problem. As a former educator, I know that even though maturity rates differ, generally by age ten the child can consciously identify what is wrong and will generally become verbal about it.

I did not have any answers for my children when they started asking questions about things, having never posed the questions to myself. Instead, they saw what was happening in our lives and watched how I lived, and each made up his or her mind as to how to respond. For a time, I believe each became very confused. They were looking to me, but even what I said was not what they saw. Everything was *not* going to be OK.

After the divorce, their father demanded that they accept him unconditionally. Each of the four answered this in a way that fit his or her personality. When he talked with my daughter, she argued with him. She still worked in the television department following the divorce and heard him tell viewers he was praying for their marriages. She disagreed with him, saying he needed to do the same for his own marriage. But she said he always answered that he would not do so, because he did not want the marriage.

When my oldest son disagreed with him, my ex-husband cut off his living allowance at college, which was another promise broken. This was an added financial burden on all of us, but we made it through. Of my two youngest, one was prone to anger and the other to confusion.

Eventually, all my children reached the same solution. They chose to love their father regardless of what he did or does, but to acknowledge at the same time that wrong is wrong. How children live with what parents do and continue to love is a miracle of a measure of God's grace that He has given especially to children. That is something we need to nurture. We need to help them fulfill the commandment to honor their mother and father, while recognizing what they have done might not be right. I tell my children they do not have to approve of what their father does or has done, but they must honor him as their father.

The maturity each of my children has shown in arriving at such a decision is something for which I can take no credit, regardless of what I have tried to teach them. Because I did not know or could not admit what was happening, I certainly did not bring any clarity into their lives until recently. One thing I did, however, was to continually point them toward God. I believe this is the most crucial issue in helping our children deal with any crisis, although it is not natural to us.

PUTTING ON A FRONT

ONCE OUR CHILDREN CAN SEE THE PROBLEM, THE NATURAL RESPONSE IS TO cover it up or to put up a front. I tried to encourage my children in the Word every day and to keep a lid on the problems. I put up a front. I fixed my children a meal each day, helped them with their homework and tried to make things normal for them. My ex-husband lived in a separate world. In earlier times, he would not ride in the same car to church with the children because he did not want to be bothered before he preached. Later he would not eat dinner with us, then he would not eat breakfast with us either. Finally he just was not around at all. Despite the mounting evidence to the contrary, I kept telling the children that everything was OK and that it would work itself out. This was a huge mistake.

God gives grace to the person who is missing the mark. But at some point that person must become responsible for his or her own actions. The person's spouse has a fine line to walk. The spouse cannot become a "cover" for sin, yet must deal with grace to allow the person time to get his or her act together. Maybe I refused to see the signs of imminent divorce because I was committed to my marriage covenant. Maybe it was for reasons less noble, like self-preservation.

I remember so well the night I recognized the cover-up I had created. I had been badgered about my pending divorce, which had not been filed, by a lawyer for five hours in a deposition that day. That night as I lay exhausted on our bed, Bob prepared to go out for the evening with his friends. I got up and dragged myself into the kitchen to make dinner for the family. But while all these things were happening, I was hearing God tell me that as long as I was in the way, my husband would not accept responsibility for his own actions. That night at dinner, I realized how much my children missed having an involved father, and I determined I was not going to put them through that anymore.

When the children were all in bed for the night, I went back into my bedroom and flung myself once again on my bed. I realized then that my husband needed to come to his senses. For that to happen, I had to stop "protecting" him. The next day was when I told him he would have to accept responsibility for his own actions and tell the church—and the kids—that he was filing for divorce.

When people exercise their God-given power of choice, there is nothing anyone can do about it. Rather than covering up crisis, the children are better off being allowed to see what is happening. Our role is not to cover, but to be sensitive and available to help them as they deal with the reality.

There is another aspect to covering up. When we do, our children can never know who we really are. We should not divulge to them every hurt we suffer nor let them see every tear we cry. Yet they do need to know we agree with what their little spirits are telling them—everything is *not* OK. If they are old enough to understand, they need to know *why* it is not OK, that it is *not* their fault and the honest truth as to what can be done or is being done to make it OK once again.

In cases where a parent has brought the trauma into the home, children often try to "get back" at the parent who hurt them by doing things that actually hurt themselves. My children's grades all suffered tremendously, starting with the year after our divorce. My oldest son suffered mostly in college. The media exposure caused him to be ridiculed for his name, and he struggled to concentrate because his mind continually wandered to his family's problems.

I remember him calling me one day to tell me he had been reading the newspaper about his parents before class began. A classmate walked up and started making conversation about how stupid and ridiculous the Tiltons were. Then she realized he was not saying anything, and suddenly remembered his name was Tilton. These were everyday occurrences for him. His grades plummeted. He could have bailed out, but instead he kept hanging in, refusing to allow the besmirched family name to rob him of his own destiny.

Then Bob and I divorced during his second year. He lost his living expenses when his father began covering only his tuition during his last two years. To my son's credit, he pulled himself together, continued to study and graduated with a degree in political science. Then he left town to make a good life for himself. I am terribly proud of him.

Children are also thrust into a position of fear, which absolutely must be addressed by the parent. My divorce came shortly after my daughter's wedding, which, even though she was an adult, filled her with fear. When she brought her fiance into our lives, they were both brimming with hopes, but he too had to deal with the emotional fallout of the tragedy.

Another fear affected mostly my youngest two children. I have said that by moving into a neighborhood without security gates, they believed we were to become open prey. The lot upon which our house was built has a good number of trees (although we never did build the tree house they wanted). When we moved in, my youngest sons kept looking out the windows to see who was coming after us.

They did not fear just people—they feared finances. They worried that we would not have enough. I thought I dealt with their fear, but I did not realize that my own actions perpetuated it. I had been cut from a sizable salary to a third of that. Then it was cut again. Then I realized the school board was going to cut me yet again. Fear set in. To make ends meet, I scrambled and ensured I was making every dime I could. But even with working seven days, I could not make ends meet—at least not the ends that used to meet.

My children noticed that we no longer took vacations as we once had done. In seven years, we have had two. Once again, they picked up signals that we were not OK. First we moved to a smaller house with smaller surroundings, then they saw me working seven days a week, then we began to make lifestyle changes to adapt to the decreased income. Unbeknownst to me, they believed we were at the brink of financial ruin.

When I quit my part-time job recently and told my children I would be home on the weekends now, one was thrilled, which I expected, but the other burst out with, "But you need that job! Aren't we poor?" When I assured him that we were doing OK, he was stunned. I am learning now how to share with them the ways in which God gives us financial blessings to build their faith, instead of fear, as well as my own.

Now I have the calm assurance that God is going to provide for us. When God does it His way, there is peace, confidence and a tremendous trust. John Osteen had said, "Jesus will be your security," and that is a resting place. I lived in that resting place for a long time. I just never expected anything to come into our lives and yank it all away. That resting place is where I longed to be again. That is now where I am once again.

Our Trauma

EVERY TRAUMA IS DIFFERENT, AND EVERY CHILD REACTS IN A WAY UNIQUE TO HIS or her own personality. My children were, and still are, exposed to things I never expected any child of mine to have to endure, and subjected to innumerable indignities both in the home and outside.

I think of divorced parents who have to send their children on "visitation" into the home of an embittered ex-spouse, or a drunk, or worse. Or children trapped in war zones, even in our inner cities, who see death repeatedly, or learn to kill themselves. My heart goes out to these children. The place to start is to cover them in prayer and ensure they know right from wrong, which will preserve them.

My oldest son is intelligent, sensitive, handsome and ambitious, but it is by the grace of God, which protected him from the things he endured as a young man. I never knew it then, and I still do not know everything, but he was subjected to horrible teasing for his morality.

My two youngest boys were in Christian school and protected to a degree, but they received their share of teasing about the "Tilton" name by other Christian students.

I always counseled my children when they were persecuted not to lash out. It was not solely the fault of those who hurt them. All four learned how to be quiet and handle the ridicule without becoming bitter or resentful, even though each was hurt in his or her own way. We developed a philosophy together that said, "That which doesn't kill me will only make me stronger."

WHAT CAN WE DO?

THE FEELING OF HELPLESSNESS PARENTS HAVE WHEN WATCHING CHILDREN GO through pain and agony is far worse than going through the pain and agony ourselves. We frantically scramble to do something—anything—to relieve their hurt and sorrow. Every day I read the Word to the ones I have at home and pray with them. We don't pray mealy-mouth prayers, but real heartfelt prayers and confessions of the Word of God. We pray for the two older children who are gone already. We often pray for their dad. Every morning we read from Proverbs during breakfast and often a devotional or another passage of Scripture. And when they do make bad choices anyway, I just walk through the consequences of their choices with them.

Children have to work out their own relationship with God. In cases of divorce, they have to work out their relationship with their other parent as well. We cannot "fix" it or tell them what to believe or how to feel. If we try, they will resent us. We cannot "fix" any part of what another person chooses to do. We cannot allow ourselves to wallow in guilt for not being able to "fix" it. Neither can we ignore the fact that it is "un-fixable."

Our requirement as parents is to let go of what our thoughts are for our children and allow God to deal with them Himself. For me, this is a heavy thing. It is very hard to go from being a "fixer" to being someone who takes a hands-off approach and lets my kids find their own way.

One of my favorite psalms reads:

> O LORD, you have examined my heart and know everything about me.... You chart the path ahead of me and

tell me where to stop and rest. Every moment you know where I am....You both precede and follow me. You place your hand of blessing on my head....I can *never* escape from your spirit!...I could ask the darkness to hide me and the light around me to become night—but even in darkness I cannot hide from you. To you the night shines as bright as day....

You watched me as I was being formed in utter seclusion....You saw me before I was born. Every day of my life was recorded in your book. Every moment was laid out before a single day had passed. How precious are your thoughts about me, O God. They are innumerable! I can't even count them; they outnumber the grains of sand! And when I wake up in the morning, you are still with me!...

Search me, O God, and know my heart; test me and know my thoughts. Point out anything in me that offends you, and lead me along the path of everlasting life.

—PSALM 139:1, 3, 5, 7, 11–12, 15–18, 23–24, NLT, EMPHASIS ADDED

In the womb, all the gifts, talents, strengths, preferences and tendencies are implanted into our children from the hand of a loving, liberal God. According to recent studies, the heart is the first organ to form. As we grow, it is up to each of us as individuals to discover what has been deposited there.

When a little boy was filled with evil spirits in the Bible, Jesus said, "Bring the boy to me." The father said the boy had been throwing himself into the fire and writhing on the ground since he was small. The young boy had fertile soil, a young field, a young heart, a young land. All kinds of things are sown into that land during childhood. The little boy did not know how to get rid of the evil spirit, nor does any child know how to cultivate the land of his heart. Jesus took authority over the spirit and cast it out. Then He told His disciples such a spirit comes out only through fasting and prayer. (See Matthew 17.)

We must teach our children they are more than just the body they walk around with on this earth. Part of our responsibility is to train our children that they have a "land" inside, a heart that belongs to God. Then we have to help guard their hearts, through fasting and prayer if necessary, until they have matured and learned how to guard their hearts on their own.

Often parents do not spend enough time to help their children find the gifts and talents hidden in their own hearts. I am guilty of that myself. One of my sons called me in the middle of the day recently and asked me what his gift was. It touched me. I told him what I saw in him, and that as he cultivates, waters and polishes those gifts, God will use him as a voice to his generation.

I know that as a single mom, I have to remind God every day—for my sake, not His—that He is in charge of my teenage boys, my older children, my son-in-law and my grandchildren. I invite Him into my home and give Him free rein to accomplish His purposes, because I know I can trust Him to do infinitely more with my children than I ever could. One morning recently when my youngest boys were going through a tremendous struggle because of their grades, I awakened in the morning in a panic, wondering what to do. But I immediately realized it was Satan trying to torment me. I told him to be quiet, asked God to take over and turned over to go back to sleep. It has taken a few years and a few trials to reach that point!

God is our children's only hope. We must point them in His direction, pray over them, teach them right from wrong and let them work it out. Although my family has had a rough ride at times, we are certainly well, whole and healthy today, even if we do still deal with reminders of our past.

One of the most precious things I have ever received came from one of my sons at my last birthday. He sent me a card that read, "You are the cornerstone of my heart."

A mother cannot hope for more.

CHAPTER 9

REPENTANCE AND
FORGIVENESS

I N MY CONFUSION, WHILE TRYING TO KEEP PEOPLE AROUND ME HAPPY, I FELT AN
emptiness inside that I had not known since I was first
saved. I did not even realize what I was feeling—it trans-
lated into an energy "to do." Sometimes I just shopped, usually
by catalog. But I could not find the right dress that would make
me feel good about myself. I bought gifts for people, but I could
not buy enough to make me feel good about myself. Things
could not fill that void.

People have surmised that I must have stopped praying to
have missed God so completely. I did not stop praying, but my
prayer life did change. As life became better and better, and I
became more self-sufficient, the intensity of my prayer life
dimmed. As the confusion grew, I got to where I could not
think straight, much less know how to pray. I mostly just spoke
the Word of God as I prayed.

Another problem surfaced. I had always journaled my devotional life. In the face of our legal battles, those journals were
subpoenaed as evidence for the lawsuits. As my most private
thoughts and meditations were read by judges and lawyers and

used in depositions to demean and embarrass me, I felt so thoroughly stripped of all my clothing and dignity that I became less consistent in journaling. When I no longer journaled regularly, my prayer life lost a great deal of power. Because of the time spent in meditation as I write, the Word becomes so much more alive to me when I journal.

REPENTANCE REDEEMS US

THE ONLY WAY OFF THE PATH OF DESTRUCTION THAT I COULD FIND WAS TO REPENT. Well-meaning teachers of the Word once taught a grace message that says we need not repent once we are saved; we need only to appropriate the blood of Jesus because our sins are already forgiven through Christ's completed work on the cross. But God clearly tells us to repent in order to be brought back into the fold. By insisting we are a Christian without repentance and continuing in our evil ways, we nail Christ to the cross again and make of Him a public shame (Heb. 6:4).

Once we have repented and entered into a covenant with God that we will never participate in that sin again, if we return to that sin we trample on the blood of Jesus. God takes our covenant seriously—His covenant with us cost Him everything.

We may have to suffer some consequences for the wrong move we made, but we need not be intimidated or discouraged by consequences. God provides grace and mercy to take us past the consequences. As fast as we can, as much as we need to, as soon as we discover our error—we must repent.

I AM SORRY

JESUS TOLD A PARABLE ABOUT A MAN WHO HAD BEEN FORGIVEN A DEBT equivalent to many millions of dollars. Yet this very same man turned around and beat another man who owed him the equivalent of only twenty dollars. If forgiveness could be measured in dollars, it would be easy to forgive others for twenty-dollars worth of bad behavior once we know God has forgiven us for millions.

In 1998 I was asked to be on a television program where, for the first time, I was able to apologize publicly. I still feel the need to ask the congregation to forgive me for being deceived into relying on my own strength instead of listening to God when I signed off on all the church assets and agreed to dissolve the corporation.

I need forgiveness from my children, the congregation and the body of Christ because I believed I was the reason my husband was unhappy and that if I compromised with him by getting the divorce over with, it would keep us all from going through more public shame. Because I did not go through the discovery process, did not confront what was happening, I settled, and the congregation's ability to have a church home was destroyed. When I compromised to cover the shame of one, I opened the door for the body of Christ to be exposed to even more shame in his second divorce.

From my point of view, I thought I was protecting the church for the congregation. Instead they lost it. I thought I was saving the body of Christ from embarrassment. Instead I brought more embarrassment to it. I thought I was protecting my children. Instead they were left with the shame of what I refused to uncover.

Some will say they need no apology. Others will say I am insincere. Regardless of what anyone says, I know that in order for my own heart to be clean and right with God, I must say I am sorry. I have repented to my children and to the congregation members I know. Today before God I repent before the body of Christ. Please forgive me.

Practicing forgiveness daily becomes a lifestyle, but forgiving ourselves is another story entirely. At one time I thought I had done something so horribly wrong that God had yanked me out of His vineyard and discarded me. We cannot move on in life when we feel that way about ourselves. If it is true, we need to repent, but we cannot wallow in it. When we allow ourselves to feel worthless, we minimize the work Christ has done in our lives. Yet, as I have seen the destructive forces of divorce in my children's lives and what the dissolving of the church has done to former congregation members—as well as the shame our name has brought to the body of Christ—I am mortified.

I listened to lawyers so much and for so long that I found myself in a vice. I was a flag-waving American patriot who could not see how people twisted the laws of the land because of my loyalty to the principles upon which our nation was founded. I believed in the people and institutions around me. I simply trusted what I had been taught about the great advantages of being an American citizen. I am sure I looked like an idiot in the eyes of legal professionals. Nowhere in a million years could I have believed people could do what they did. It was not within my scope of understanding.

DEALING WITH THE PAIN

WHEN OTHERS HURT US, WE OFTEN RUN FROM GOD, ESPECIALLY IF WE ARE HURT by one who is considered God's ambassador. I have heard about people who were so hurt by what happened at our church that they actually left the faith. The best thing I did was not run from God, yet the only way I could run *to* Him was to repent and forgive.

A heart full of bitterness will keep us from God's blessings. It is easy to hang on to anger and resentment because someone threw us in a pit and walked off, leaving us bleeding and hurt—just as they did to Joseph thousands of years ago. But our Lord is the Good Shepherd who will leave ninety-nine others to come after us. When we run to Him, He comforts us and pours oil in our wounds. He is our redeemer and deliverer, the One who lifts our heads.

Forgiveness washes out our spirits, freeing us from the

bondage of bitterness. If Jesus is living and abiding in us, and we in Him, then we have the ability, power, right and authority to forgive because He forgives. When people say, "I can't forgive," they deny the power they have from abiding in Jesus.

In the uneven emotions and cloudy rationale of fighting too many battles on too many fronts, I made the best decision of my life. I think it is a decision that can change the course of any life. Let me outline that decision for you.

DIVORCE!

EVERY DAY UNTIL A WEEK BEFORE MY HUSBAND ANNOUNCED OUR DIVORCE, HE told me he loved me. I do not remember him ever missing a day, even during the most turbulent times. Every year he greeted me with flowers for our anniversary. I do not remember Bob ever missing a year—except our last. From every trip he brought me gifts. I do not remember him ever forgetting to bring a gift from a trip. Even after the *PrimeTime Live* television program, he replaced the diamond in my wedding band with a larger diamond he had chosen himself. Men who traveled with him always reported to me that my husband never looked at another woman—never. Regardless of any differences between us on the surface, I always believed that from deep within his heart sprang a well of undying love. Certainly I felt that in mine.

Any odd behavior that he exhibited I easily understood. The *PrimeTime Live* broadcast—and the resulting media attack—had greatly upset my husband. He entered a period of deep depression—even to the point of threatening suicide. For days on end he sat in the dark in his green chair in the master bedroom, staring into the darkness and listening to the golfers outside as they yelled mocking comments toward our home. He repeatedly said, "I'm on the edge." I prayed for him often, and as I prayed, God seemed to be telling me that he was in worse shape than anyone knew. I thought God was indicating his condition regarding the pressure he was under—not his condition regarding the other life he had started.

I tolerated every form of inappropriate behavior that came in the aftermath of the *PrimeTime Live* telecast, including what I see now was an increased disrespect toward me. He was frequently absent from home, but seemed to have legitimate destinations, and although I raised an eyebrow occasionally—and sometimes my voice—I just thought he was dealing with the stress his way, and I was dealing with it my way.

No one was more surprised than I was when he went through with what he had been threatening for weeks—a divorce. He had made two empty threats about divorce to me in recent weeks, but on August 15, 1993, he announced to our church that we would be separating and divorcing. From what I have heard since, most of the congregation believed he meant divorce was a consideration, but that we were really just separating. But we all picked up our morning newspapers the next day, and I read along with everyone else that he was to file that Monday morning following the church announcement. In the paper was a photo of me from the archives in the church art department, which had never been officially released for the media to use. Someone had taken pains to ensure the newspapers got the story right and got it early.

A few weeks later, at the end of September 1993, I sat in my office at the school building adjacent to the church, stewing over all that was going on. We were now in the waiting period before the divorce was final. I still bore the brunt of the ongoing court battles—but was now without the support or companionship of a husband. Mulling over my situation and filled with self-pity, suddenly the Holy Spirit spoke to my heart in the form of a question, "What are you going to do?" Then I heard the Lord answer His own question, "I require you to walk in love and forgive him."

Immediately my emotions rose up. *WHY ME? Why did I have to be the one to forgive him? What about the "man of God" pastoring the church next door? Why wasn't God telling him what he should do?* As emotions bubbled up, I knew I should not be anywhere near the home we had shared together—or him. Hurt and angry, I called a friend and asked her to fly to Newport Beach, California, with me—my favorite place of rest. I quickly traded airline mileage for the flight and secured a hotel room. A friend agreed to watch the children. When I arrived, I bought the book *Bad Things Happen to Good People* by Robert Schuller. We stayed two days.

The first night, I read Dr. Schuller's entire book. On the second night, I became serious with God. My friend had gone to sleep, but I pulled back the drapes at the hotel room window and had a silent conversation with the Lord as I watched the fog roll in from the ocean a mile away. *How could You put the responsibility on my shoulders to walk in love? How could You do that to me after all I've been through?*

I knew the Word of God. God says:

> Vengeance is mine; I will repay, saith the Lord. Therefore if thine enemy hunger, feed him; if he thirst, give him drink; for in so doing thou shalt heap coals of fire on his head. Be not overcome of evil, but overcome evil with good.
>
> —ROMANS 12:19–21

I knew God's command not to sin against our neighbor. But if someone does sin—stealing from the neighbor, tricking him, slandering him, moving his property marks—that person has not only sinned against the neighbor, but against the commandments of the Lord. (See Leviticus 19.) The neighbor who has been sinned against could take vengeance into his own hands instead of giving place to God's wrath. But if he moves out of the way, God will bring His own wrath upon that individual.

If I did not turn loose and give my hurt and anger to God, I knew I would stand in the way of God, hindering Him from bringing about the repercussions for wrongdoing. God had already spoken to my heart that I must allow Bob to feel responsibility for himself.

For many hours I paced in silence, rehearsing the previous years in detail, tracing what went wrong, trying to reason why my husband could simply discard me as if I were unimportant to his life or his life's work. I knew he was unhappy, understandably so, with all we were going through. But I had never known he was unhappy with *me*. I knew he was unhappy with my working too hard—but it never occurred to me that his complaints meant he was unhappy with the whole marriage. Hadn't I done everything he demanded, to the point that it hurt my own conscience? I had never asked to become our ministry's general manager. He delegated that job to me. It was my part of the partnership we had formed. Hadn't I done it to the best of my ability for him, for us, for God?

I Purposed in My Heart to Forgive

During that pivotal night in a California hotel room, I met God while staring out into the fog. I knew that I did not know what was happening in any other person's heart. But I knew I could control what was happening in mine. I had to decide to walk in love...or not. To forgive...or not. God's Word clearly pointed out that if I chose not to forgive, I would strap myself to a life of bitterness. But facing the need to humbly forgive everything that had ever happened seemed no different than looking down the barrel of a gun to commit suicide. Truly I would have to die to my flesh to do it.

> For if you forgive people their trespasses [their reckless and willful sins, leaving them, letting them go and giving up resentment], your heavenly Father will also forgive you. But if you do not forgive others their trespasses [their reckless

and willful sins, leaving them, letting them go and giving up resentment], neither will your Father forgive you your trespasses.

—MATTHEW 6:14–15, AMP

If I did not forgive Bob, I would not only keep him in bondage, but I would also willfully be held captive. If I did not forgive him, the Father would not forgive me my trespasses, and I could not be blessed by the hand of God.

I thought about my Bible friend Joseph. Joseph ran from the temptation of Potiphar's wife, but he was accused anyway and thrown into prison. Joseph was as human as anyone, but we never see signs of unforgiveness in Joseph's life. He had to work through a lot of things. Knowing his own brothers started the whole mess must have been horrible. I know how he must have felt. I could not understand how friends could do this to me, or why. God raised up Joseph to become second in command of the entire nation and blessed Pharoah's house because of him. Joseph chose to walk in the ways of his Father, and God blessed him.

I struggled with God all night in that hotel room. *What had I done that was so wrong?* Early in the morning, I quietly watched the fog rolling back to sea. "I surrender, Lord, and submit to You," I said. "I purpose in my heart to forgive him and do my best to walk in love toward him."

I returned to Texas from that pivotal date with God. My husband called to say he needed to come by and get the divorce decree finalized. We were discussing the various points of the divorce decree when he suddenly said, "I don't know why I'm doing this, but while I have the courage, I'm going to do it."

I told him I had gone away to California and struggled with the Lord, who required me to walk in love toward him. "I forgive you," I said, "and I've purposed in my heart to walk in love toward you."

At that point, it was a commitment. I had no idea all there was to forgive. But it did not matter. It was the best decision of my life, and it has contributed more than anything else to my being a whole, happy person today. It feels like death when you make the decision, yet it results in the best life of all.

To walk in love means to walk with the presence of God in your life because God is love. To walk with God requires walking in love, regardless of what others have done.

Forgiving in Advance

As I looked out into the fog and talked to God that night in California, I thought all I had to forgive was a divorce. But I later discovered that forgiveness is a process. Written in the margin of my Bible next to the following verse is this comment: "October 2, California."

> And having said this, He breathed on them and said to them, Receive the Holy Spirit! [Now having received the Holy Spirit, and being led and directed by Him] if you forgive the sins of anyone, they are forgiven; if you retain the sins of anyone, they are retained.
>
> —John 20:22–23, amp

I believed that if I did not forgive my husband, his sins would be *retained,* meaning he would be locked in the state he was in. Regardless of how hurt I was, I did not want to see that happen.

As I stared out into the fog, remembering all the ugly incidents of the past few weeks, I knew then that choosing to forgive my husband did not mean I was admitting I was wrong and the others were right. Nothing could justify the reprehensible behavior of a few who called themselves "Christians" around me. Forgiveness does not mean we agree that we deserve what we get. Forgiveness just allows us to be free from it.

"Be not overcome of evil, but overcome evil with good" (Rom. 12:21). In the Old Testament God said not to engage in the sins of the land. In the New Testament, the apostle Peter says that we should not have anything to do with people who sin against God. (See 1 Peter 2.) That means *get out of there!* Sometimes we cannot flee from the situation, and in those cases Jesus said to forgive everyone "seventy times seven" (Matt. 18:22). He instructed us to:

> Rejoice not when thine enemy falleth, and let not thine heart be glad when he stumbleth; lest the LORD see it, and it displease him, and he turn away his wrath from him.
>
> —PROVERBS 24:17–18

As we pray for our enemies and forgive them, we make room for God to move on our behalf. Others may have dug a pit for us, but God says they will fall into it themselves. When God visits His wrath upon the wicked, we are not to slap high fives and call our friends to say, "I told you so." We pray for our enemies and take our hands off so God can do a work of restoration. Enemies need an intercessor if they are ever going to be free.

> Love your enemies, bless them that curse you, do good to them that hate you, and pray for them which despitefully use you, and persecute you; that ye may be the children of your Father which is in heaven: for he maketh his sun to rise on the evil and on the good.
>
> —MATTHEW 5:44–45

MORE FORGIVENESS NEEDED

OUR DIVORCE WAS FINAL ON OCTOBER 18, 1993. I REMEMBER THE DATE because Bob wanted to finalize it on a Friday, which was Amy's birthday. I insisted we postpone it until the following Monday so she would not have a negative memory associated with her birthday.

In the summer of 1994, as I struggled on my side of the street, the Lord told me to write down my feelings and everything I needed to forgive. I forgave my ex-husband once again for hurting the church people, for hurting our children, for divorcing me, for leaving me alone to walk through the treacherous mess, and I forgave the woman I suspected might be his new wife. In the middle of a hot afternoon on July 6, 1994, I took a friend, crossed the street and got down on my knees in front of the sanctuary at a little flower bed. I dug a hole and wept as I read the list aloud. Then out of my mouth came, "Thank You for allowing me to work in Your vineyard. It's not mine or Bob's. This vineyard belongs to You." And I tore up all those words on that little card, dropped it in the hole, buried it and walked away. As far as the money and assets that were left in the church, I released all claim to them. It all belonged to God, and I figured that God could retrieve it.

My husband secretly remarried in February 1994. Amy called her dad's home from time to time, and a woman occasionally answered, but he offered no explanation other than having friends over. Finally, in his depositions during the lawsuit against the television network, he had to admit he was married. He called the children and me late in January 1995 to tell us of his marriage before we heard it on the news. My children had clung to the hope that their dad would come to his senses and restore our home until they received his call.

He wrote a letter to his entire mailing list saying he had met the woman of his dreams during his darkest hour, and she had administered "healing love" to him. Then he came back to Dallas and stood in the church my family had built to say God had given him a new family, which did not include our four children. It was very difficult for me and very hurtful for our children. If I had not learned to walk in forgiveness, I could have killed the both of them.

For me now, the issue was not merely that I had to forgive him—I had to forgive her, too. Forgiveness is not mushy or wimpy. Misguided love or sentiment is gooey stuff that "loves" people without addressing any issues and has no strength. Forgiveness does not hide truth, but addresses the truth in the love of God and forgives because Jesus said to forgive. Nothing is stronger.

We forgive not when we are asked, but before the other person knows what they have done wrong or even thinks of asking for forgiveness. God forgave us before we asked for it, because He sent Jesus for us. God raises the beam by saying we must forgive others in order to receive Christ's forgiveness (Matt. 6:15). We forgive, but if it is only going to cause hurt or confusion, we do not have to tell that person we forgave them.

Years later I saw cars pulling off the highway to go into the parking lot of our former church building. When I saw those cars I remembered that hot afternoon on my knees at that flower bed. God reminded me of my words, "It's not mine or Bob's. This vineyard belongs to You." Those cars streaming into that parking lot were like God's banner written for me: "Yes, the vineyard is Mine, and there is still a harvest to be picked." I was thrilled to see God's hand still upon that place and people still gathering in His building to worship Him, even though the earthly leadership had changed.

In Luke we read these words:

> Pay attention and always be on your guard [looking out for one another]. If your brother sins (misses the mark), solemnly tell him so and reprove him, and if he repents (feels sorry for having sinned), forgive him. And even if he sins against you seven times a day...you must forgive him (give up resentment and consider the offense as recalled and annulled).
>
> —Luke 17:3–4, amp

The Bible says to forgive others and let it go. The people we forgive are not necessarily the people we restore, but in our forgiveness, we release them to be restored.

We may even have to forgive people for doing "nice" things. When I stepped into the position of general manager at the church, I was told to do so. Later, I was accused of trying to take over because I filled the position I was asked to fill. This may sound silly, but I need to forgive people for their accusations. People may need to forgive me for just doing my job. My ex-husband may need to forgive me for acting like his "mother" and enabling him to get himself in a mess, or for fighting his battles for him. My children may need to forgive me for trying for so many years to "fix" things for them.

The day I walked through my forgiveness by burying that list, I was still in the middle of destruction, but I immediately felt a great sense of release. My incentive had been that I did not want to see Bob in that condition. I wanted, and still want today, to see him as a man of God, as a father who loves, protects and nurtures his children and puts them above himself, his desires and his friends.

By freeing him through my forgiveness, I freed myself as well. From then on I felt no emotion whatsoever when I saw my ex-husband or his wife.

I put a tape by Dr. Edwin Louis Cole into the tape player in my car so my boys would get something out of it as I drove them to and from school. Instead it hit *me*. One day after I dropped them off, it was near the end, so I left the tape playing. In a powerful moment, Dr. Cole told the young people in the audience to come to the front. Then he stood in the place of the person who had hurt or molested them and said, "I'm sorry. It should have never happened. You are not the problem."

I wept as I heard those words. I had never allowed myself even to think it, but in that moment, I realized I had longed for someone to say, "I'm so sorry this happened to you and your kids; I'm so sorry that we hurt them. I'm so sorry you were left in the heat of a battle to stand by yourself, to fight for yourself. You were not the problem." The desperate, unspoken craving of my heart was answered with Dr. Cole's words on the tape. Four years after I had put my pain in the hole outside the church, I now completely released the past and let it go.

THE GREAT KILLER

AS I HAVE FORGIVEN, MY MIND HAS BEEN WASHED OF HURTFUL WORDS AND angry memories. The slate has been cleansed. It has been hard to remember incidents for this book—not because I buried them, but because I exposed them in the marvelous light of God's love and grace, in whom is no shadow of darkness. As I exposed the memories of the bleakest hours to God's love and light, they have disappeared, and the pain of them has vanished.

Once we forgive others, Jesus can forgive us. Then we can forgive ourselves. Forgiving myself took longer than forgiving anyone else. I thought I had been thrown out of the vineyard...I thought I had committed heinous sins. I could not come to grips with the fact that I had allowed financial freedom to pass between my fingers. I felt so responsible for being so deceived that I could not imagine how God could ever use me again.

As I realized each mistake I had made, I asked the Lord to forgive me. This started immediately after the divorce and has continued to the current day. I felt so guilt-ridden that at first it was easier to say everything was my fault than to admit my husband of twenty-five years no longer loved me and had gone off to live another life.

I went through the Scriptures to read about church leadership and sin, and I realized I was not guilty of some of the heinous sins. I realized that I had not sinned flagrantly or turned my back on God as I been led to believe. As I read the responsibilities of a husband, including loving me as he loved himself, I was strengthened. I started to realize that it was not all my fault.

From time to time as I shopped or ran errands I would meet up with a man who had been on the church staff. When the church folded and he lost his job, he was so bitter. Any emotion I ever felt never came close to his. I encouraged him to forgive and get on with his life. He never did. Now, years later, he has done almost the same thing his former pastor did.

If we do not forgive, we cannot release the sin. We can end up doing the exact same thing. The hurts, pains and memories of the past keep us in prison—not a cement-and-stone prison, but one of real bondage. Unforgiveness can keep us from moving, much less walking into the future God has for us.

Why don't people get back on the right path? Often it is because of guilt. Guilt is a killer. People are unable to forgive themselves, thinking their failings have been unforgivable. Wallowing in their guilt, they miss what God has for them.

I knew a man who had an affair with a married woman. His guilt was so great he could never fully forgive himself, and his life never rebounded into what I believe God had for him. This "mark" on his spirit was well within God's ability to heal, *but he could not accept the healing.*

Years ago I wrote in my journal that if we believe, even for a split second, that God is behind what goes wrong, we lose all power to resist the enemy. That is where I ended, feeling that God was angry and disappointed with me, that He had brought all this wickedness on me to stop me. Jesus said that if we repent and ask forgiveness, He will forgive us and cast our sins into the Sea of Forgetfulness. I realized that if He will do that for us, who are we not to do it for ourselves?

> Who is a God like unto thee, that pardoneth iniquity, and passeth by the transgression of the remnant of his heritage? He retaineth not his anger for ever, because he

delighteth in mercy...and thou wilt cast all their sins into the depths of the sea.

—MICAH 7:18–19

For seven years, I have had to judge my own heart to repent and try to figure out how I made certain decisions. I know I can never live apart from God's presence again. I know that He is in my life and guiding my footsteps. I do not want to be one step away from Him—ever. To draw close to Him, I have to do what He does—forgive *me*.

I do not accept responsibility for everything that happened, but I deeply regret my decisions and what followed them. What I did wrong could have been corrected had there been an opportunity. But what I did wrong was still what I did wrong. And for that, I have learned to forgive myself.

CHAPTER 10

IT IS TIME
TO MOVE ON

WHAT WOULD YOU HAVE LEFT IF YOU LOST EVERYTHING—ALL YOUR money, possessions, power and influence? Who are you without those things? I have discovered a powerful truth: You can *never* lose everything.

A title does not make you a person. It is only a title—you are still a person without it. A home does not make you a person. It is only a house, not a part of the people who live in it. A bank account does not make you a person. It is only money, not a part of the person who decides how to spend it. You are a person without any of these things. You were uniquely created. And you can move on to life beyond these things.

An entirely new life awaits you, as it was awaiting me. And although claiming the new "land" where God takes you can be difficult at times, you *can* conquer it.

For those who experience trials of all kinds, our loving Father always provides a way out—a way of escape. God has provided a way out for you. Choose life!

I have set before you life and death, blessing and cursing:

130

therefore choose life, that both thou and thy seed may live: that thou mayest love the Lord thy God, and that thou mayest obey his voice, and that thou mayest cleave unto him: for he is thy life, and the length of thy days.

—Deuteronomy 30:19–20

Jesus suffered our depression, shame, sin, illness and death so we could live. Giving our emotions to God may be the hardest thing to do because of our own feelings of unworthiness, but it is time to nail all those emotions to the cross of Christ and allow Him to complete the job in our lives that He came to do.

If we are serious about learning the way out and pressing through to victory, the very first step we must take is to choose life. The way of escape is open, and it is available by going through. But we cannot start until we choose life.

When tragedy, disaster, devastation or ruin come our way, the worst emergency exit we can take is suicide—escaping from life altogether. Sometimes it takes every ounce of energy just to get up in the morning. I have said, as many have, "I hate this life." But if we can keep dragging ourselves out of bed each day, calling out for God's mercy, seeking Him through His Word and prayer, we can be assured that God will pierce the darkness. Eventually His grace will give us a moment of opportunity whereby we can emerge back into the light of His love. Many people accept the darkness as the way they will live their whole lives. But when the moment comes, and God's heavenly flashlight illumines the way out of the pit, if we have cultivated our hearts even during our distress, we will come through.

I would have been the last person on earth to say that I wanted to commit suicide, but the darkness became so unlivable that I certainly wished I could die. Yet I refused to be the one to administer that final blow to my children. For a time, it seemed that was my only salvation.

TUNNEL VISION

AS I CONTINUED WORKING AT THE SCHOOL AFTER THE 1993 DIVORCE, THE DARK tunnel closed in around me. It was the "Tunnel of the Unknown," the "Future Without Security," the "Mess I've Made." I went in courageously, believing God would be with me in whatever I had to go through and that I would come out the other side into His glorious light.

One day in that dark tunnel, I did make a decision. Late in 1996, I decided not to live in the tunnel any longer. It was a simple decision on my part, but it took three long years to make it. Once I chose life, God started moving heaven and earth to give me that life.

Because I left my marriage with designer clothes, a Mercedes Benz, a new home in the suburbs and child support, people assumed I had walked away with half the savings of the entire church. They did not know that they were looking at what I ended up with—there was little more. I was so gun-shy by that time, I was not even sure that I would receive the court-ordered child support I had been promised. Everything else was gone. If I did receive it, I wanted to bank it for my children, so I kept working as if it did not exist to see if I could make it on my own. No one knew how fortunate I felt to have come away just with what I had. It should have been better, but it could have been worse.

After the divorce, the church's lawyer obligated me to work with a realtor to show our home so it could sell. This was terribly difficult while I was working full time and still raising two young children in the home, but I did it anyway. I agreed on the condition that the realtor remember that we could not move until my new house was ready. The lawyer did not require the realtor to hold to that agreement, and two weeks before our house was ready, we were forced to move into a hotel, then move again. That additional move cost me dearly.

I was only allowed to take from our former home those items we had personally purchased, which did not include the furniture. If I wanted any furniture, the church's lawyer said I would have to buy it from the church.

I put some of the furniture I thought I would like into storage at one of the church's buildings when we moved into the hotel. When I went to pick it up two weeks later, a suspicious-looking man—who said he was the new church administrator—asked in a hostile tone, "Can I help you?"

Although I was allowed to move that furniture into my new home, the church's lawyer called and badgered me continually about paying for it. As I moved it around and tried to settle it into place, I finally realized the size of the furniture dwarfed my new home. It was simply meant for a larger house. So I returned it. The harassment was not worth it, and I did not need the painful memories the furniture represented. One of the church's staff members told me later that they set the furniture out and invited the staff to take whatever they liked—*at no charge.*

I know that my situation was not nearly as difficult as that faced by many single parents. My heart goes out to all single parents, especially mothers who leave their opportunity for a career behind and do not have the financial base or their youth with which to start over. Family laws allow a little child support each month to feed and clothe a child, but in most cases, that amount barely provides enough money for the parent to hire childcare while working. If God will show me how, I have purposed in my heart to do something to help others relieve the difficulties of single parenting.

THE PROCESS

ANYONE WHO HAS GONE THROUGH CRISIS KNOWS THAT JUST ABOUT THE TIME IT seems as if it cannot get any worse, it finds a way of doing exactly that. For years I felt as if I had fallen off the Empire State

Building, and as horrified as I was to know I was falling, I just could not reach bottom. When my fall was arrested for a moment, something else would push me, and I would free-fall down some more floors.

Pressure has a way of magnifying our trials and troubles. As we stand in line at McDonald's, we feel the stares of the other people in line. We think, *Everyone knows!* It is the same feeling we have when we have toilet paper stuck to the bottom of our shoes and do not know it! But everyone does *not* know. Even if your name has been smeared across the newspapers from coast to coast and around the world, everyone does *not* know. And what they think they know just might not be right anyway. Often we are just reacting to the pressure, which is magnifying each stage we are going through.

After a trauma such as death or divorce, certain natural, emotional, spiritual issues must be dealt with one by one. Obviously for me, I had to deal with a big case of *denial.* After denial, the cycle continues with *anger, grief* and, finally, *acceptance and getting on with your life.*

"I just want my life back!" was my cry during the denial stage. As the denial wore off, the anger surfaced. "I'm so mad at the devil for throwing up another hurdle for me to 'fix.'" I was mad at a few other people, too. Then came the grief. "God, please, this is not how my life was supposed to end up!" Finally came acceptance, and when it came, with it came courage.

In the Bible is a story of four lepers who were within the walls of Jerusalem during the time it was being besieged by a foreign army. (See 2 Kings 7.) Jerusalem had completely run out of food. The lepers knew they were either going to die of their leprosy, starve or be killed by the invaders. They weighed the situation together one evening, deciding which option was the worst. The enemy was encamped just outside the walls of the city, with regular supply lines bringing them plenty of food and water. The lepers finally reasoned that since they were going to die one way or another, it was worth the risk to sneak into the enemy's camp for food.

When they ventured outside the city to check out the camp, not a soul was to be found. At first they thought it was a trick. However, unbeknownst to anyone, God had driven the opposing army into a fear so great they had fled, leaving all their goods behind. As the first to discover the spoils, the lepers ate their fill and then alerted the leaders in Jerusalem, and everyone was able to enter the abandoned camp for food. Instead of dying, the lepers turned out to be heroes.

Like the lepers, when it seems that we have been dealt certain death, we have to weigh our options. It may be the death of a business... death of a reputation... death of a marriage. One option is just to sit day after day, feeling horrible about ourselves. Or we can complain about it to such an extent that we alienate our friends and lose our own hope. Another option is embracing our troubles as our "lot in life" and determining never to leave, even if the door is flung wide open for us. Or we can assess the situation and, in a burst of courage, get up and march forward.

GIANTS!

As I FOUND THE COURAGE TO MARCH FORWARD, I HAD NO CLUE OF WHAT I WAS going to find. I was entering a "new land," one completely unfamiliar to me. As I read His Word, God showed me that when you come into your new land, enemies will need to be conquered. Before the Israelites entered Canaan, they sent spies in to the land. The spies found giants. When the Israelites finally found the courage to go into the Promised Land and face those giants, the giants all fell under the hand of God.

I studied the giants God named in His Word to find out what they meant to my life. The "giants" we face today are not made of flesh and blood, but are principalities and powers under the control of Satan. They use other people, our own emotions, our imaginations and our circumstances to do their dirty work in our lives.

Just as He revealed the giants in the Promised Land to the Israelites, God has already revealed these giants to us.

> When the LORD your God brings you into the land which you go to possess, and has cast out many nations before you, the Hittites and the Girgashites and the Amorites and the Canaanites and the Perizzites and the Hivites and the Jebusites, seven nations greater and mightier than you, and when the LORD your God delivers them over to you, you shall conquer them and utterly destroy them. You shall make no covenant with them nor show mercy to them.
> —DEUTERONOMY 7:1–2, NKJV

After naming the giants, God said two remarkable things: He said they were more powerful than us. But He also said that He would hand them over to us to conquer, and that when we did, we were to completely destroy them.

As I studied these giants and God's Word regarding them, the certainty of God's Word washed over me like a refreshing bath in crystal waters, perking me up and giving me strength to defeat these enemies in my new life.

Through their school, my children had met a youth pastor whom they really liked. Because of their interest, I had begun attending the church pastored by Lawrence Kennedy. I went to church after studying these giants, and Pastor Kennedy said, "We're going to start a study today on the giants in the land." I am using some of his notes to expose these giants, so you can utterly destroy them, too.

New attacks—the Hittites

The first giant the Lord listed is the Hittites, people who brought fear and terror into the lives of others. Hittites threaten us. They growl at us and demean us. They scream at us. "You aren't anybody!" "You are a nothing!" "How will you ever manage to work and raise those children?""You aren't strong enough to make it!""What will you ever do that will bring in the finances you need?"

When we hear such things, it is easy to give in to the enemy, scream at God and run *from* Him instead of *to* Him. I disciplined myself to run to Him even though I could not feel His presence, see Him or hear Him outside of knowing that He was speaking directly to me through the Word I read. The heavens seemed to be shut to me for the first three years after my divorce. I had only a fragile thread of trust left that His Word was true and that He would never leave me nor forsake me.

For me, this was my survival. I saw nothing in the natural that made me feel better. All I could hear while I worked at that school were the Hittites screaming at me through lawyers, parents of school children, school board members, former friends and strangers.

Coming under the attack of the Hittites causes a continual downward spiral of hopelessness and despair, which results in having no hope for a future. One of the first scriptures through which God spoke to my heart as I went through this ordeal was from Jeremiah.

> "For I know the plans I have for you," declares the Lord, "plans to prosper you and not to harm you, plans to give you hope and a future. Then you will call upon me and come and pray to me, and I will listen to you. You will seek me and find me when you seek me with all your heart. I will be found by you," declares the Lord, "and will bring you back from captivity. I will gather you from all the nations and places where I have banished you," declares the Lord, "and will bring you back to the place from which I carried you into exile."
>
> —Jeremiah 29:11–14, niv

Fear points us toward the negative. If we meditate on faith, we will attract that for which we have faith. If we meditate on fear, we will attract that which we fear. Faith says we can have what we believe. Fear says we can have what we are afraid of. God wants us to operate in faith, not fear.

The enemies that are hurling fear and terror at you *are not* from God. When everything in your life has fallen apart and you are caught up just in trying to keep your oars in your boat, it is easy to listen to words that try to deceive you into thinking that all this is "from God." But fear is not from God.

> For God has not given us a spirit of fear, but of power and of love and of a sound mind.
> —2 TIMOTHY 1:7, NKJV

> Such love has no fear because perfect love expels all fear.
> —1 JOHN 4:18, NLT

You may not be too confident about anything that is going on in your life, but you can come confidently against this enemy of fear and intimidation and say, "No! I will not be afraid. My God said He would never leave me nor forsake me. He will be with me. He will give you into my hands this day!"

Greed—the Canaanites

After the divorce was over in 1993, the phone calls from the church's lawyers began, informing me the church would not support the school or pay my salary. Everything continued to be yanked from me, taken away, chipped at and eroded. Fear engulfed my life. *How will I ever make it? What will I do to make a living?* were my constant thoughts.

Nothing I did that had always worked before could help the school financially now to offset what we lost in church support. People within the school seemed to expect me to finance it personally, assuming I could. I did put some school functions, sports equipment and the like on my personal credit cards and credit line, hoping to turn a corner eventually and pay myself back.

With the headlines working against me, I had a hard time finding people who would risk the liability to help me form a school board so we could incorporate the school separately from the church. Once I had a board formed, the members did not always stay. One left without explanation. Another said his business partners were pressuring him to resign. Still another, who remains a great friend today, simply could not keep up the schedule with everything else he was doing. A stream of well-to-do businessmen passed through the board, yet to my knowledge, only one ever made a financial contribution. I became the school's largest contributor, giving back a portion of my salary. Everyone agreed that it was a great Christian school, but it seemed that no one really wanted to work for it.

Toward the end, Christian businessmen and ministers offered to buy certain assets of the school, but only at a loss, which we could not afford. To enlist more help and support, one of the board members tried to develop a group who would help raise funds, but even some of them complained that it was my fault the school was not attracting more new students. With all that was going on at the church across the street, it was a wonder we were able to maintain the level of enrollment we did for each of the four years after 1993. Church membership had plummeted to the low hundreds, while school enrollment maintained a steady several hundred children.

I am certain that terrific, well-meaning people crossed my path during this time, but I was so overwhelmed that I never saw them. I felt like a duck in a shooting gallery, making a job of traveling back and forth on the same path and constantly getting hit.

While I oversaw and managed the school, I still worked on all the lawsuits and the IRS audit to help the church without pay from the church. When I went to court, I would testify to the principles by which we had operated in the past, but I could no longer in good conscience testify about the character of the people involved.

I did not know it then, but both at the school and in the law-suits, I had encountered *Canaanites,* people who are downright greedy and covetous. *Covetousness* is wanting what others have, thinking you deserve it more than they do.

Through the parable of the rich fool, Jesus told us clearly not to be ensnared by greed.

> Then someone called from the crowd, "Teacher, please tell my brother to divide our father's estate with me." Jesus replied, "Friend, who made me a judge over you to decide such things as that?" Then he said, "Beware! Don't be greedy for what you don't have. Real life is not measured by how much we own."
>
> —LUKE 12:13–15, NLT

It was important for me to continue to believe that if I was faithful in tithing and giving, God would "open the windows of heaven" and "pour out a blessing so great you won't have enough room to take it in!" (Mal. 3:10, NLT). God continued by saying:

> "Try it! Let me prove it to you! Your crops will be abundant, for I will guard them from insects and disease. Your grapes will not shrivel before they are ripe," says the LORD Almighty. "Then all nations will call you blessed, for your land will be such a delight."
>
> —MALACHI 3:10–12, NLT

When we lose, or stand to lose, all of our "things," that loss threatens our security. It can cause us to start grumbling about God's giving other people what it does not seem they deserve. I was almost led down that road by the very Canaanites whom I was trying to fight. Canaanites entice us to look at others in comparison to ourselves. It is never difficult to justify in our minds that we deserve to have what others have. Although I did not want more "things," I certainly wanted to hang on to what I had. I had to be willing to let go of everything and trust God completely—or the Canaanites could have caught me.

Instability—the Girgashites

The Girgashites were unstable, double-minded, confused and filled with unbelief. They were people who lived in the marshland and were always defeated by their enemies. The confusion I had experienced as a result of compromise years earlier was nothing compared to this giant of instability I would face during this period of my life.

Reading *one* legal document is enough to confuse many of us, but being immersed in a web of legal technicalities with people giving me differing advice at every juncture was thoroughly confusing. Unfortunately, I lost a few rounds against this giant before I recognized it for what it was. When I did recognize it, with God's strength I started to annihilate it, washing my mind with the Word of God to regain some clarity.

In crisis it is easy to become confused, to be indecisive because you are unsure of which way to turn. It is very, very easy to begin believing that there is no answer for your situation. These are all natural thoughts, but we cannot stay there. In Texas we say that birds may fly over our heads, but we do not have to let them build a nest in our hair.

Adam and Eve lived in complete innocence with all their needs met under God's covering in the Garden of Eden. Their world fell apart when they gave in to the deceiver. Where they had once known only the goodness of God, now they had to face both good and bad. They had to work hard with their hands and birth children in sorrow.

Even in that crisis, God did not leave Adam and Eve wondering what to do. God had already provided a way to restore them into right standing with Himself and to give mankind the ability to conquer the deceiver.

King Nebuchadnezzar in the Old Testament also once lived in a place of peace and provision. In the early years of his life, he never knew the depths to which a human being could fall. But as he rose in power, he made the mistake of taking credit for all God's blessings. As a result, God banished Nebuchadnezzar from the kingdom, driving him out of society to eat in the fields on his hands and feet like an animal. One can only imagine how he felt seven years later when his mind came back to reality. When it did, he was reestablished as head of the kingdom with even greater honor than before.

In trying times—times of crisis—our only stability is God. He alone can restore us to a place of honor. Even when we have ruined things ourselves, God is willing to restore us—and not halfway, but all the way to a place of honor.

Lost boundaries—the Perizzites

When we are cast away and questioning God, it is easy to run to the world. I have always loved ballroom dancing, so after the divorce I went with a group of friends from time to time. I went on a few dates, too. But I just did not fit. I never did anything I could not admit to my children, but I did flounder around wondering how to be a single person.

I did not know how to function as "one" instead of "one of." Little things perplexed me. Sitting in the church auditorium with a row full of children next to me, I struggled over which box to check on my tithes envelope. *Am I a Miss? Ms.? Mrs.?* How could I be anything but a "Mrs." with all those kids? The only real change was that a piece of paper declared me *divorced.* I decided the last thing I needed to do was pursue being a "single." I just needed to redefine my boundaries and be a mother to my children, so I checked "Mrs." God would be my husband and a father to my children.

I did not realize that the Perizzites were closing in on me. *Perizzites* are people who never built their boundaries. When we are under attack from the Perizzites, other people can influence us. My dark tunnel experience was only prolonged because of the people to whom I listened and the opinions and perspectives to which I agreed. What a snare!

People around me seemed to fall left and right to this giant, being influenced by and influencing others. The school was losing money monthly, but instead of trying to help, the people on whom I depended started hurting the situation. When the headmaster resigned, two remaining teachers decided I was a detrimental factor for the school. One morning they walked up and down the hallways of the school, using their influence to urge all the teachers to stage a walk-out in protest of my presence. They did not seem to care about the children in the classrooms.

God enabled us to overcome that disaster. We hired a new headmaster, Dr. Richard Swetnam, who was one of the finest educators I have ever met. Every day Dr. Swetnam stood out-side to greet the children and parents as they arrived. Probably everyone thought he would soon give that up, but even when cold weather came, there he was every day, donned in his stocking cap, gloves and a big smile to welcome the kids to school. What a giant in God's kingdom.

Even with so much to endorse him, because he attended a mainline denominational church that taught slightly differently from us, soon after he came, some of the parents started a whispering campaign against him. It did not seem to matter that he knew all the children by name and also had a business mind for school administration, which was a great asset to me. His kindness and ability eventually quieted the whispers.

As he settled into his new duties, our accreditation became due with two separate accrediting bodies. One entity gave us our accreditation with little struggle. But the other accreditation team came on campus and grilled the headmaster about his religious beliefs. Then they grilled me about...well...*being me*. I believe they may have cast doubt in the minds of some of the board members about my ability to carry on because I *was* me. This was very disheartening. But I could not very well wave a flag and say, "Hey, look at me, I'm doing a good job even in the midst of this crisis, and I haven't done anything to send me to jail!" I could not do that, but I could fight those evil influencing spirits in the spirit realm—and so can you. You will see God win a victory for you.

Pride and arrogance—the Amorites

The Amorites were proud and arrogant people who made their homes in the mountains. Pride is one of the easiest giants to spot, and one of the hardest to overcome. God said, "The pride of life—is not of the Father but is of the world" (1 John 2:16, NKJV) Pride is the result of the Fall of man, and "pride goes before destruction, and a haughty spirit before a fall" (Prov. 16:18, NKJV).

Pride wants to be approved by others and brings strife, confusion and contention. (See Proverbs 29:23; 13:10.) Pride becomes a chain that binds people up. (See Psalm 73:6.) God hates pride! (See Proverbs 8:13.)

What do we do when someone does not like us? If we find something wrong with them or talk badly about them, we might be dealing with pride more than anything else. My pride was certainly wounded, but as I began to realize what a "giant" it was and how much damage it could do, I started letting it die as it was attacked. Recognizing that we can do nothing of ourselves apart from the grace of God is one of the first steps toward dying to that pride. If we feed pride, we are going to take a fall. And we never know how far there is to fall until we are falling.

Crises seemed to come in wave after wave during those years at the school, including two accreditation probes, the attempted walk-out, personnel changes, constant turnover on the board and the money squeeze, which we could not resolve. Then one day the church's lawyer called to inform me that our gym had been sold. This was not good. In order to be part of the school system through which we were accredited, we had to have a gym. We went everywhere looking for a gym to rent, share, buy—anything. But there was nothing. The worst part for me to deal with was the fact that Bob and the attorney knew the critical nature of the necessity for a gym.

One of the only things I had fought for and received from the agreement I had made with the church's lawyer was a piece of property that the church had purchased on which to build the school. When I finally got the deed from the lawyer, the transfer of it was based on the school's becoming a legal nonprofit entity within two years. The lawyer knew it would likely take longer, and probably expected the land to revert to church control. But instead, when I applied to the IRS for non-profit status, I received it within three months. You know your life has turned upside down when it is the IRS that saves you!

I knew we needed that property because the church had only agreed to house the school for five years. We would have to relocate somewhere. But when the school started being stripped of support, I went to bank after bank to try to borrow against the value of the property. Because the headlines were still full of reports about the lawsuits, the banks said they could not be sure the church would not lose all its assets in one of those suits and come after our property. The school board finally put the property up for sale because we were so strapped for cash. But even the sale would not go through because, again, in the minds of the public, the school was still a part of the church—which was in the newspaper continually.

Eventually the sale went through, and with the proceeds of the sale we were able to purchase our gym back from the man to whom the church had sold it. This man owned a company that did work for the church—and still works with my ex-husband today—so I had some suspicions about the whole transaction. But we needed the gym to stay alive, so we did what we had to do.

It was not long before the headmaster and I put our pencils to paper and realized that the school was not going to survive. The best thing we could do was close it down at the end of the school year and let the parents have some warning to find other schools for their children. I had struggled to keep the school going for almost four years since the divorce. It was time to concede.

Lies—the Hivites

The Hivites lived in the lowlands. They represent liars. "Hivite" threats were leveled against me that tried to make me believe that God did not care about me and my children; God was so displeased with me that this mess I was in was what I deserved. I believed that for so long. Those lies just about pushed me over the brink until I stood up to that giant and said, "No more."

Sometimes we feel we are too far gone and do not have the energy to conquer giants. But if we have God, He will strengthen us. Perhaps we are afraid we will not make it, or that God is not with us. Perhaps we feel He is mad at us, or maybe we have bought into one of these lies that everything that happened to us was our fault. We do not have to listen to the Hivites' lies! If God says He will hand the enemies over to us, even though they are stronger, then He will surely do it.

The devil himself is a liar. The Bible says he "does not stand in the truth, because there is no truth in him. When he speaks a lie, he speaks from his own resources, for he is a liar and the father of it" (John 8:44, NKJV).

The only way to defeat this enemy that even God says is "more powerful" than us is to run to what we know is true,

God's Word. The Bible says that "every tongue which rises against you in judgment you shall condemn" (Isa. 54:17, NKJV). I kept thinking *God* would condemn them, but as I recalled His Word, He said that *I* could condemn them. I had to discipline myself to believe His Word and to believe that no matter what was said about me, from friend or foe, God would defend me and bring me back one day to a place of honor.

Depression—the Jebusites

The lies of the Hivites went hand in hand with the last enemy, the "Jebusites," who are people who are downtrodden and depressed. I am not a naturally depressed person, but the darkness became so pervasive around me that I wanted to give in to this giant, curl up and die. As nice as it sounded, I had four children looking to me, and I could not do that to them. I had to carry on.

A few months after the divorce, the cross-examination against me in the courtroom was so grueling and hateful that it moved even my ex-husband to tears. During one recess, he came to me and apologized for what he had done to me. Those tears had more in them than I realized at the time, because unbeknownst to me, he was already remarried. But I accepted what he said in the spirit it was given and refreshed my determination to walk in love toward him. At least he still had some heart!

Certain things I knew I could change as I pressed on, but some I could not change. I could not change the fact that I had become involved in another lawsuit. One of the school parents was also a lawyer—one of the good kind. He advised the school board that if we did not file a lawsuit against the church, then we were not fulfilling our fiduciary duties, and the parents of the school children could sue us. So we filed one. I added my own charges against the lawyer who defrauded me in the side agreement at the time of my divorce. It seems crazy when the only way to avoid a lawsuit is to file one!

At some point, before the headmaster and I discussed the fate of the school, I had a dream that the school was dead. Feeling warned by God in the dream, I continued doing what I could, but I started removing myself from situations and people. The headmaster and I presented our findings to the school board, recommending they close the school. They rejected the suggestion. That was when I resigned—July 1997. By the time the lawsuits settled in early 1999, the board had been forced to close the school due to low enrollment. In the meantime, I had moved far down the road.

YOU CAN CONQUER THE GIANTS

TODAY, IN ORDER TO GET OUT OF A DARK TUNNEL, WE HAVE TO DECIDE ONCE AND for all that God did not put us there, and He does not want us there. It is *not* our "lot in life" to live there. Then, one by one, we have to start fighting the giants as we emerge into the light. Always remember, God will help anytime we ask Him.

As we conquer the giants, one of the biggest to start with is the Perizzites—the negative influences around us. We have to cut ourselves off from people who negatively influence us as well as music, films, books, anything else—perhaps even newspapers.

To claim the land God brings us into, we have to plow that land and plant new crops. We must read the Word every day and write out our prayer requests to bring before Him every day. I write scriptures on index cards and carry them everywhere. Whenever one of those giants comes along—fear, pride, insecurity—I just read my card, saying aloud what God's Word says about me. Giants cannot stand when we do that. The enemy has to flee the moment we resist him. (See James 4:7.)

Remember that we cannot move into every new territory all at once. We have enough on our hands fighting one battle at a time. Some battles are not even worth fighting, so choose them carefully.

God has commanded us to annihilate those giants, wiping

out even their memory. Run the enemies of God off your land. Reclaim the boundaries of your land. Put up fences and post signs: "Keep Out!" "No Trespassing!" "This Land Belongs to God!" Slay your giants!

WHERE'S THE ARMOR?

SOMETIMES WHEN AN UGLY THOUGHT PASSES MY MIND, I HAVE TO SHAKE MYSELF and say, "Come on! You're an ambassador in the kingdom of God. You cannot afford to act in selfishness, or it will be death to everything you've received. You cannot break covenant with God!"

Just because my ex-husband was wrong does not give me the right to compromise. It is entirely too easy to say, "Well, the man of God blew it, so I can, too." No one going off the deep end justifies us following.

I have the utmost respect for the ministry and the men and women who lead ministry today. I watch Christian television, read Christian books and listen to Christian tapes every day. I have been inside ministry and outside ministry, and I have seen the worst as well as the best. Many men and women are truly called of God to ministry. There is no reason to get in a huff about one minister or another. We need to keep our eyes on what Jesus has for us and follow Him with our whole hearts.

> If you need wisdom—if you want to know what God wants you to do—ask him, and he will gladly tell you. He will not resent your asking. But when you ask him, be sure that you really expect him to answer, for a doubtful mind is as unsettled as a wave of the sea that is driven and tossed by the wind. People like that should not expect to receive anything from the Lord. They can't make up their minds. They waver back and forth in everything they do.
>
> —JAMES 1:5–8, NLT

> Tell me clearly what to do, which way to turn.
>
> —PSALM 5:8, TLB

Paul called himself Christ's ambassador and applied this term to all of God's ministers, which in those days meant all of God's people. Wherever Paul went, he took over, even if he was not the one in charge. He took over the prison as a place from which God's kingdom could be launched. He took over the island where he was shipwrecked as a new part of God's kingdom, winning the indigenous people to Christ while he was there. I like what Bishop Eddie Long says:"Don't take sides; take over!"

The apostle Paul wrote:

> Be strong with the Lord's mighty power. Put on all of God's armor so that you will be able to stand firm against all strategies and tricks of the Devil. For we are not fighting against people made of flesh and blood, but against the evil rulers and authorities of the unseen world, against those mighty powers of darkness who rule this world, and against wicked spirits in the heavenly realms.
>
> Use every piece of God's armor to resist the enemy in the time of evil, so that after the battle you will still be standing firm. Stand your ground, putting on the sturdy belt of truth and the body armor of God's righteousness. For shoes, put on the peace that comes from the Good News, so that you will be fully prepared. In every battle you will need faith as your shield to stop the fiery arrows aimed at you by Satan. Put on salvation as your helmet, and take the sword of the Spirit, which is the Word of God. Pray at all times and on every occasion in the power of the Holy Spirit. Stay alert and be persistent in your prayers for all Christians everywhere.
>
> —EPHESIANS 6:10–18, NLT

One morning during my regular devotions, I was still on my first cup of coffee when I read about the armor of God. Suddenly I realized I had lost my armor. I got right up and started preparing for the day, putting on my clothes piece by piece, naming each piece after the armor of God, arming myself spiritually against any onslaught the day might bring. Now I do it on a regular basis.

The armor of God starts with the *belt of truth,* meaning the actual facts and the spiritual reality that God's Word is the final authority. God's Word is truth and eternal, and every one of His righteous decrees endures forever. In Bible days, a man belted his waist, tucking up his robes to prepare for strenuous activity. The belt of truth braces me with sincerity and reality to stand against lies and hypocrisy.

The breastplate of righteousness is named for the wide metal piece that protected the warrior's heart. Righteousness is the just and right, whatever conforms to the will of God. We become in Christ all that God requires us to be, all that we could never be in ourselves.

The shield of faith is the firm persuasion and conviction of God's authority based upon hearing His Word. Faith brings the invisible God into the physical realm and produces trust in what we cannot naturally see.

Our feet are shod with the preparation of the gospel of peace. Shod means "to bind." Gospel means good tidings of salvation through Christ to be received by faith on the basis of Jesus' death, burial, resurrection and ascension. That means we have bound the gospel to ourselves.

The helmet of salvation refers simply to a hard hat. Salvation is a deliverance, a preservation of eternal deliverance from the bondage of sin. We are not conformed to this world, but we are renewed in our minds, which protect us.

The sword of the Spirit is literally the spoken Word of God. A sword probes the conscience and subdues the impulses of sin. The Spirit, like the wind, is invisible, immaterial and yet powerful.

Every morning for years I had put on my armor, but then for years I stopped. Of course my shield had big holes blown through it by the time I found it again. I had to repair the armor, blow off the dust, beat the dents out of my helmet, straighten out my sword and find my shoes. I had been clothed only with the belt of truth, because I had never left the Word of God.

Everywhere my feet go, the Good News now goes with me, bringing hope to hurting people. My helmet is on; my mind is secure in the Word of God. The fiery darts of the enemy cannot pierce through to me. I have taken up the sword of the Spirit and the shield of faith. I am ready to live again!

I have learned that whenever trouble comes my way, I can let it be an opportunity for joy. For when my faith is tested, my endurance has a chance to grow.

So let your endurance grow, for when it is fully developed, you will be strong in character and ready for anything.

CHAPTER 11

REBUILDING THE WALLS

R ECENTLY AS I RACED MY DIRTY, OIL-DEPRIVED CAR AROUND THE bend on Interstate 35 in Farmers Branch to hurry home, traffic suddenly slowed, and I was stunned to see the freeway exits jammed. Police officers were directing hundreds of cars into already-crowded parking lots surrounding the buildings where I had once copastored a thriving congregation. Built as functional, practical facilities, the prefabricated exteriors seemed to have weathered the years about as well as I had. I discovered that T. D. Jakes had rented the four-thousand-seat auditorium for a series of services. I thought, *What a thrill to see what I helped build and dedicate to the Lord utilized once again for His glory.* Seeing those crowded parking lots brought back a flood of memories! Those years of ministry were wonderful, fulfilling years when I felt the Lord's pleasure.

Whenever we are in a crisis, with all the conflicting emotions we experience, it is important to find out what we have lost, what is left and what we will need to rebuild. This is what each staff and church member needed to do in the years following the church's collapse. In the aftermath of the divorce, it was important for me to offload negative emotional clutter, physical bits of the past and even negative people. But that took a very long time to understand.

SORT IT OUT

FOR ME, THE FEELING OF FALLING PERSISTED FOR YEARS. INSTEAD OF WAITING UNTIL I hit rock bottom, I finally realized I needed to get on with my life in some way and start sorting out what I had or did not have. The first step was to get rid of the cobwebs in my mind. We wonder what might be hiding in them or what is around the next corner.

When fear creeps in, look out! It may be fear about finances, fear of the future, fear of family and relationships or fear of death. To move past fear and into faith, we have to make time to reflect calmly and look at what is real. We cannot hope to find time in that downward slide, but we must make time to sit and pray and accept anew that God is our source.

Life keeps us far too busy for a devotional life just to happen accidentally, and crisis only makes it worse. We have to make an appointed time every day. I like to get up before there is any movement in the house whatsoever and spend time with God, talking to Him, telling Him how much I appreciate Him. Clutter has to be removed from our schedules to give God time and to thank Him for the sacrifice Jesus made for our lives.

A dream I had during the time I was sorting things out took on special significance for me. The dream was a simple one—a dog was caught in the cobwebs under some furniture in my house, and I could not get it out. As I struggled to free the dog, my ex-husband came into the house, then immediately left. As I ran after him for help, I saw a woman in the car trying to hide as they drove away.

The significance I felt attached to the dream was profound. Those cobwebs represented the webs of destruction that had overtaken my life. They had hidden every sign of life—even the dog. I felt that those webs had covered everything I was or had or had lost or could gain. And Bob was no longer available to help me—indeed, he had a hidden life away from me.

Have emotional cobwebs invaded your life? We have to clear the cobwebs so we can find out what is left. Have you looked for the "spoils of war"? Just as in the story of Jesus' multiplying the loaves and fishes, like the little boy who had a sack lunch, everyone has something. We can *never* "lose it all." Find your "spoils of war"; find what you have left. As we give what remains to Jesus, He will bless it and return it to us so we can willingly give it away to someone who needs it. In that way, one day we will watch what was meant to destroy us turn to blessing and begin to multiply.

REBUILDING FINANCIALLY

I HAVE EXPERIENCED MANY FINANCIAL STRUGGLES AND A FEW OUTRIGHT failures—when we launched into ministry and ended up building fences (about all we knew to do), when we lost everything in the satellite network and had to pay off over a million dollars of debt and when I found myself as a single mother with an uncertain financial future.

I conquered the fear of man, but I still had to deal with fear—fear of financial failure. Being a single mom has been difficult for me, but it has not been the struggle of many single mothers. My children do not have a "deadbeat dad." Their father has continued to meet the requirement for providing child support for our children's benefit. But the stipulated support could not provide them with the same lifestyle they had before the divorce. At first we had no luxuries—in fact we did not even have many of the things to which we had become accustomed—so I allowed myself to feel pressured to make up the gap.

I worked seven days a week for a few years, which bothered me because my children were growing up and I was missing out on much of their lives. My checkbook told me I could not stop, and I was certainly not too lazy to work, but my heart nagged me. One day as I was driving, the voice in my heart became so loud that I fairly shouted, "OK, I'll resign my second job." That was a step of faith for me. The Lord started blessing me financially. An amazing peace settled over me as I listened to Him speaking to my heart, enabling me to step out in faith. For all my work, I had not added one thing to my family's welfare. All I had done was prove again to myself that I cannot do it alone. But when I began to walk in faith, God began to prosper me.

We can work hard, we can strive hard—but God is our Provider. God is Lord of all, including our finances, or He is not Lord at all. Our financial future is dependent upon God and His blessings. This I know: Fear God, not finances. When we exercise faith in God and His Word, He will bring us through.

How do we rebuild what was lost? God promises to restore what the "cankerworm," or crisis, destroyed. When I went to Florida to move my personal belongings out of that house, I was still thinking Bob was not serious. We were divorced, but I did not understand it. As I finished the last run through the house and backed the car out of the driveway, I hit the garage door opener and watched the door slide down. I said aloud, "This chapter in my life is closed."

At that point, I had to take assessment of what I had. I had nice things, although not enough to fill a house—but I had the basics. Many people walk away without even the basics. A lot of people come away from a crisis with nothing. I felt that if I could get a business or career going again, I would make it. There was a long time, and many more flights to fall down, between having that "knowing" in my heart and seeing it begin to happen.

If we have taken inventory of what we have, and determined

what we need, then we can start to throw out the trash that has built up while we were not paying attention. Clutter keeps us from seeing our way to where we need to go. Take finances as an example. For years as my downward spiral continued, I kept thinking, *How am I going to provide for my kids? How am I going to buy a decent car when this one gives out?*

Rather than getting out my bank statements to look at my money—or lack of it—to evaluate what I had so I could create a strategy for getting where I needed to go, I pretended instead that nothing existed. I threw my statements into a pile and never looked at anything until I had to at the end of the year.

When I finally started really looking, I realized people had taken advantage of my "Tilton" name, either out of fear or for profit. My auto insurance premiums, for example, were higher than those for the average person. My agent took it up with the head office, proved that I was a safe risk, and they reduced my premiums. This came after I had paid ridiculous rates for six years. If I had taken stock earlier, I might have avoided the high premiums. It is very important to start the process as soon as possible.

As we sort through and discard the truly unnecessary clutter, we can count our blessings as we see more clearly what is left. But a word of caution—it is easy to throw out the wrong things, things that bother us, but that we should actually hang on to. That is why we should stay focused on the Lord and not let those cobwebs cause us to think wrong.

Our lives will not immediately rebound as we go through this clutter-clearing process, but if we will also clear out our cluttered schedule and stay in the Word, God will deliver us eventually.

The Bible says, "If you fail under pressure, your strength is not very great" (Prov. 24:10, NLT). Dr. Cole says, "Pressure always magnifies." Pressure makes the lightest straw seem like something that can break a camel's back. Then the slightest problem—a glass of spilled milk or a long line at the bank—can devastate us. We need to clear out the cobwebs and clutter. Then we can take an objective look at our situation. The creativity may be gone...pressure may have fried our brains so we cannot think...life may have dealt such a deadly blow that we are filled with discouragement...and we may finally recognize that we are not the "strong" person others may think we are. But in discovering those things, we will discover one overwhelming fact—we need Jesus every day. That is the beginning point to wholeness for each of us!

WE CANNOT GO BACK UNTIL GOD SENDS US!

GOD DELIVERED THE CHILDREN OF ISRAEL FROM EGYPT, BUT WHEN THINGS DID not go their way, or they encountered difficulties, they were frightened, angry and wanted to run back. They thought of the one good thing they had had in Egypt—a variety of foods to eat—whereas now they had only manna. They forgot that as slaves they had been held captive against their will, beaten and unable to become the people God had created them to be. They became irritated, unforgiving, self-centered and impatient. They even left God for a golden calf they created.

Like the Israelites, we have to fight the temptation to run back. Going back to the past prevents us from overcoming what we find in the now, which will lead us to what we will have in the future.

> Love the LORD your God...obey His voice...for He is your life and the length of your days; and that you may dwell in the land.
>
> —DEUTERONOMY 30:20, NKJV

> Be strong and of a good courage, fear not...for the LORD thy God, he it is that doth go with thee; he will not fail thee, nor forsake thee.
>
> —DEUTERONOMY 31:6

Before we turn our lives to God, we live according to what we think is OK. Some of us do not do as many "wrong" things outwardly as others. But all of us are doomed to an eternal death, worse than anything we experience on earth. According to the Bible, we are in fact already wearing graveclothes. Believing in Jesus leads us into eternal life, so we no longer have to live with death. The spiritual graveclothes fall off piece by piece as we allow Jesus to become our Lord in each area of life.

These enemies of the past can surround us, yell at us and convince us that we are not worthy to be redeemed and useful for kingdom work.

God gives us the tools to fight the giants who would throw graveclothes back on us. He says to submit to Him first and foremost (James 4:7). You may struggle to do that because you find it difficult to trust anyone or to have the faith to give yourself over to God. God's Word says, "Faith cometh by hearing, and hearing by the word of God" (Rom. 10:17). Faith grows as we read what God has to say about us.

Once faith starts to grow, we have to step out and put legs to our faith. God's Word tells us:

> I can't see your faith if you don't have good deeds, but I will show you my faith through my good deeds. Do you still think it's enough just to believe that there is one God? Well, even the demons believe this, and they tremble in terror!
> —JAMES 2:18–19, NLT

As our faith begins to grow, we have to work on our minds. We will never get where we want to go if we do not discipline our minds to take us there. "Don't copy the behavior and customs of this world, but let God transform you into a new person by changing the way you think" (Rom. 12:2, NLT). The Word of God is like a big scrub brush that cleans out our minds as we read it. God says to cast down imaginations and everything that exalts itself above the knowledge of God (2 Cor.

10:3–5). We pull down anything that is contrary to God's Word, including worries and fears, and bring them captive into the obedience of Christ. That just means we choose to believe God's Word about that worry or fear, or whatever it is.

> You were his enemies and hated him and were separated from him by your evil thoughts and actions, yet now he has brought you back as his friends...the only condition is that you fully believe the Truth, standing in it steadfast and firm.
>
> —COLOSSIANS 1:21, 23, TLB

We have to fight not to fall back into our comfort zones, wrong relationships or negative actions or attitudes.

STEP OUT OF FEAR

AFTER MY DIVORCE, MY CHILDREN AND I MOVED OUT FROM THE "BUBBLE" AND learned to live like normal people. We packed up and moved into our lovely home in a new tract.

I never announced I was coming, but everyone in the neighborhood knew I was there. It was a pleasant surprise to them that I was quiet, not an outgoing, flamboyant person. My next door neighbor says people still ask her about me, even ten years after the *PrimeTime Live* telecast. She tells them I am a terrific cook and a great neighbor. Bless her! The greatest stir I created was when I decided plantation shutters were easier to maintain than curtains, so I had shutters installed in all my windows.

For a long time my sons and I were watched and monitored. Someone even sat outside our house with a satellite dish to pick up sounds inside. (Where do people get these ideas?) The most provocative things they would have heard were my boys arguing or me yelling, "Get your homework done!"

Stepping out of fear and into faith was like a homecoming for me. If a headache persists for a while, then stops, you suddenly realize how irritating the ache was. That is how it felt for me to go back to a place of real dependence upon God. What a sweet, wholesome, wonderful place that is. We can either step out in this kind of faith or live in fear. Where fear lodges, there is no room for faith. Fear drives faith away.

The children of Israel escaped from Egypt, but they were trapped at the Red Sea with the Egyptians hot on their trail. The path under the Red Sea was there all along, but it took Moses' lifting his rod, symbolic of the Word of God, and the people's stepping into the sea by faith for that dry pathway to be uncovered. (See Exodus 14:13–18.) It is the same for you today. Step out in faith where God directs you, and you will find the way out. The path God prepared for you is there.

Some people never make it through obstacles in life because they never deposited in their hearts or wrote on their minds the Word of God. We have something like a bank account in our spirits. If we have deposited the strength of the Lord Jesus Christ, He will pick us up and carry us through with His strength. When we run out of ourselves and all we can do in the natural, we find we can truly depend on God to carry us through in the supernatural.

There is no security in the natural realm. It can all be gone today. We can have millions in the bank. We can live in mansions. We can have yachts that float on the highest sea and the deepest ocean. We can have servants who stand around waiting for our command. But it can all be gone in a day. Then we are back to square one. It is either you alone, or you and God.

Lost Friendship

In the types of crises that test loyalties, we often lose the best friends we ever had. In my case, through divorce, I lost someone whom I had once considered my very best lifelong friend—my husband.

For many of the early years of our marriage, Bob and I were

each other's closest confidant and friend. We did everything together, even things one of us did not especially like. I was never taken with the great outdoors, but we had enjoyed many outdoor adventures together. On the domestic side, he scarcely knew his way around a kitchen, but he always sat at our table admiring and bragging on how I had set it while we hosted dozens of dinner parties.

We had always had our differences. He likes adventure, living the lifestyle of an Indiana Jones. I cannot imagine a life more exciting than Martha Stewart's. He got a kick out of running out the door on the spur of the moment to ride go-karts or explore a new restaurant. I was overjoyed when I perfected my recipe for chicken velvet soup. He loved bouncing along the water in his boats. The only time I like boats is when they are tied to the dock. But we had loved each other.

Being opposites, for years we had fit together perfectly. He was the visionary; I came along to fill in the details. It was only when others started driving the wedge between us that our differences began to look insurmountable. He wanted to learn how to scuba dive, and I would not go to the lessons. I wanted to play tennis, but he would not learn how.

I realize I was probably not the best wife. I actually *enjoy* doing my duties. I do not think a day has gone by in the last thirty years that I did not cook, unless I was away from home. Even at the height of our media troubles, I enjoyed sitting down to dinner each night and being able to look each of my children in the face and find out how they were doing and what was important to them. Chasing any other kind of lifestyle was not important to me. What mattered most was to have my family around me so that together we could fulfill our destiny.

Toward the end, we entered into such conflict. As I look back on it, it is no wonder I was confused. My husband told me every day he loved me, but he also called me dumb. He said I hated people and was mean to employees, yet he refused to correct anyone himself and said he appreciated me for doing it. His lawyer said he deserved everything we had ever built, but he himself said we were equal partners. During the time I was still attending the church before our divorce, sometimes he would stop the whole service and have a healing service. As usual, people would really, truly be healed. He would say things like, "No man could do this unless God was with him." And I would sit there thinking, *Well if God is with him, He is acting contrary to His own Word.*

In the course of the crisis, I had to come to grips with the fact that I had lost the person I had cared for most in life. He was unique. But he was not mine. To this day, no one I know who ever knew him speaks badly of my ex-husband. My friends and I have compared notes, and whenever we meet up with someone from the "old days," all of them talk with great appreciation about how much they learned, and all of them say they are still praying for him. I am, too.

Give Your Shame to Jesus

Sometimes we are so ashamed, so embarrassed, so mortified that we do not want to go anywhere or try anything. God is *never* ashamed of us. No matter what we do or what we did, He "maketh not ashamed" (Rom. 5:5). We can take all our shame and, as hard as it may be, give it to Jesus. He already took all that shame for us onto Himself so we could live free.

Having your name smeared through the media seems as if it would bring shame. But the great mistakes I made in the legal situations I faced far surpassed the media's cause for shame.

Much of the shame I felt came from knowing that in the midst of all the chaotic noise of what was going on in my life, I had failed to hear that still, small voice of God to guide me in some of the decisions I had made. All the other voices in my life had taken preeminence. I became so accustomed to people taking shots at me as I went to and fro. For a while, "bad guys" were all I could see. All people seemed to be gossips, backbiters, robbers and disloyal friends. I could not hear what the "good guys" were saying. Many "good guys" around were not speaking out themselves because they were cowed or squelched by the people who were shooting arrows at me. I felt boxed into a dark hole filled with the screams of accusation.

I had to get out into daylight, away from the screaming voices, before I could really hear the affirming whispers of the "good guys"—or of God—again. Once there, I learned how to do what I could each day and let God take care of the rest.

You may never have faced—or ever will face—what I have faced. But you may feel the shame of letting other voices crowd out God's voice. Jesus already took your shame—and my shame—so we can live free. I had to really grasp that truth, but when I did, it set me free—and it will do the same for you.

BUNNIES, BLANKETS AND BUBBLE BATH

BACK WHEN WE HAD THE CHURCH, AFTER MORNING SERVICES WERE OVER ON Sundays, I generally hung around to talk with people, then strolled across to the nursery and children's church area to retrieve my children. I loved the people, and I loved being with them.

Without the church as the center of my social world, I almost became a hermit. I holed up in the school office. Each day I would go to work, possibly to depositions or court, back to pick up my children, then home to make dinner, supervise home-work, do laundry, work out and fall into bed. Until we found a church that would embrace us, my children and I visited different churches, but we often felt uncomfortable. My friends said my personality had changed by this time—I had become guarded. I did not laugh as easily as I once had. They said they always saw pain in my eyes. What they were really looking at was a woman who had become a victim, then a survivor. When

I finally resigned the school in 1997, I realized I needed to stop *merely surviving.* It was time to *live!*

I love people, and I love giving gifts. My friends laugh at me because they say my entire face lights up when I think of a gift for someone. I know my pulse races. When someone told me recently that they were giving a dinner party for single mothers, I did not hear another word they said. My mind raced over what I had at home that I could give. I set to work making gift baskets for each of her guests. I have met famous people and gone on safaris and been to the White House, but nothing gives me a bigger thrill than finding the perfect gift for myself or for someone else to give.

My ex-husband and I had sent gifts each year to an enormous list. In addition, the church gave many gifts. It seemed there was never a day without a birthday, anniversary, wedding, new baby, graduation or holiday that required a gift. According to the way the lawyers had required us to structure our finances, the church paid for our housing. But we paid for everything else—including entertaining, cars and gifts.

In order to be a little economical, I had decided to start my own business and to buy gift supplies wholesale. But the church's lawyer said I could not do that because it would cause a conflict of interest. Even though I would never have charged the church to make a profit, because of the quantity of supplies I would be purchasing to supply gifts, it was believed that I would have gained the intangible benefit of having a higher percent discount. Instead, the lawyer's wife had a business of sorts through whom we ordered everything. In retrospect, it is odd that we were not allowed any benefits, but the lawyer who had just as much of a vested interest was allowed to do so.

After the divorce, while I was still administrating the school, I incorporated a gift business to work at part time. By that time, my salary had been cut from the church and I did not know how long the school could afford to pay me, so I signed up with Mary Kay and a host of other sales-oriented businesses, hoping one or another would work out for me if the school could not pay me. If it was moral and legal, I tried it.

Then I left the school in July 1997. I had been convinced by this time that even though I had managed a multimillion-dollar company, I was dumb. I so thoroughly believed no one else would want to have anything to do with me—or my business skills—that I spared myself the embarrassment of being turned down for executive positions and threw myself into my gift business instead.

I made contacts through the Chamber of Commerce and referrals, which brought in a great profit until the end of the Christmas season of 1997. Then the gift season stopped, and I did not know what to do next. I decided that certain gifts could be sold all year, so I contracted with a nearby mall for the year of 1998 for a small tiered cart. I filled the cart with monogrammed bags, christening gifts, picture frames, gourmet coffees and other treats, like stuffed bunnies, baby blankets and bubble bath.

Moving my business into the mall was a huge decision. My ex-husband's second divorce was making headlines. What his lawyers had feared I would do in our divorce, she was doing... many times over! Oh, the embarrassment and shame it brought my children as they watched the evening news. I really wanted to stay home in bed with a pillow over my head—not expose myself to more public ridicule. But I also wanted to be out with people again. I did not want to hide. I did not want to run. I wanted to learn how to *live*.

Like the lepers in Jerusalem, I weighed my options and thought, *What else could possibly happen?* All people could do was yell at me, and I had already become used to that! I took a deep breath and took my place in the middle of the mall, right across from the Electronics Boutique and Gap Kids, in full view of everyone who walked by on the first or second levels. There, for all to see, I stood by my little cart stuffed with gift items.

I took with me my trusty index cards, which I used to meditate on the promises God had given me from His Word. When I did not have a customer, which happened often between holidays, I would study my cards. Though my head was down, I could feel people looking at me from all angles, trying to decide where they had seen me, if they knew me or if it was really Marte Tilton. I cannot imagine the things that must have gone through their minds. No doubt most everyone believed I was guilty of some heinous crime or that I was out on parole. They probably thought I was doing community service while on probation. Maybe they thought someone had felt sorry for me and given me a minimum wage job at their cart.

But whatever people thought, many wonderful people said many wonderful things. Not a day went by that someone did not come up to me and say, "It's nice to see you," or "I've prayed for you." What a refreshing turn of events!

Just once someone said something that hurt me—but it was not the words that hurt. During the week before Mother's Day, I noticed some teenaged boys smirking at me from the doorway to one of the stores. In a few minutes one of them came over, maybe on a dare, and bought something for his mother. As he was leaving he said, "I just feel so sorry for you."

I took a deep breath and finished the next three hours of work. Then I dragged myself out to my dirty car and unleashed the torrent of tears. I cried all the way home. I had steeled myself against ridicule, but pity hurt much worse. It hurt that people viewed me as a victim. Probably it was my pride that was hurt too, which was OK anyway.

In that mall, I found that I did not have to look very far to find people who were much worse off than me. Watching people, I found much for which to be grateful. I saw people in wheelchairs or with missing limbs, and I would thank God that although my legs were tired from standing all day, at least I had legs to stand on. One day I saw a little girl, approximately seven years old, who had a discolored arm that was ten times its normal size. My heart was moved toward her, and I prayed silently for her even as I praised God for my children's health. Often I saw people who were living with life-or-death situations far worse than mine. When it comes down to it, as much as anyone in crisis hates to hear trite statements, it really was a blessing that I had my health and my children, and nobody had died.

People's opinions of me started to change. Some people started saying again, "Marte, you're so strong." Others, behind my back, were surely saying, "Marte is so stupid." I did not know what to believe about myself. If I were so strong, why did I go through this at all? This much I did know—God had brought me out from that dark tunnel, and I was determined to get my life back. I did not feel like facing another day, much less facing a bunch of people. But neither did I want to fail. So I got up and started moving, just doing what I could each day.

LOOKING BACK

AS I STOOD IN THAT MALL, I REFLECTED BACK ON THE STUPID DECISIONS I HAD made. I could have gone through the courts with my divorce, even though it would have pulled everyone else through the media spotlight as well, and possibly damaged my children even more. Instead, in a way, I had just given in to the badgering and belittling I was getting from the opposing side. By making the decision I had made, I had lost so much for my children's future.

I thought about Joseph a lot. Joseph would not allow himself the luxury of self-pity, bitterness or fantasy. He could have easily given in to the victim mentality, but he rejected it. In the end, God blessed everything Joseph did. I wondered, *If I keep believing God, will it turn around for me?*

One day at the mall, I was drinking my morning coffee from

my favorite mug and reading an article about the divorce between my ex-husband and his second wife. I did not subscribe to the newspaper myself, but a friend had given me the section with the reports from the day before. No one had been more surprised than I was when my husband divorced me. This time, no one to whom I talked was surprised at the revelation of that news report—except me.

I set my coffee on the cart and read it again. My ex-husband, it was reported, admitted to adultery with many women during his two-year-long second marriage. This was not the man I knew. My coffee grew cold—just as I did—as I sat mulling it over.

Like Joseph, I had the opportunity to become bitter and unforgiving. But because I had made my decision to walk in love, instead I started feeling compassion for my ex-husband. I could have hated men. I could have hated ex-husbands in general. I could certainly have hated lawyers. I could have hated preachers. In fact, I could have hated God. But I knew none of those emotions would produce anything positive in my life. They would just drag me down into the pit and lock me up in darkness for life. So I gave it all up to God and set my hand to the plow to work in the new land He was giving me.

Keep On!

God does not bless evil and arrogance. Greed can never bring God's blessing, so greed has to be cast down from our minds. Wise Solomon said, "A greedy person tries to get rich quick, but it only leads to poverty" (Prov. 28:22, NLT). He continued by saying, "Greed causes fighting; trusting the Lord leads to prosperity" (v. 25, NLT).

Jesus said:

> You are not defiled by what you eat; you are defiled by what you say and do!...It is the thought-life that defiles

you. For from within, out of a person's heart, come evil thoughts, sexual immorality, theft, murder, adultery, greed, wickedness, deceit, eagerness for lustful pleasure, envy, slander, pride and foolishness. All these vile things come from within; they are what defile you and make you unacceptable to God.

—MARK 7:15, 20–23, NLT

I do not want—and have never wanted—tainted money. I would rather make a living by learning how to work on cars, for which I have no natural ability, than to take stolen money. But I did want to gain the money won by the fraud case to give my children and me some financial security for our future. I was deeply disappointed that I did not. I was more disappointed in myself, because I had compromised again. When I had the opportunity to fight, I had backed off with concern over the old IRS bogeyman bringing me grief if I did end up with the money. It seemed that every time I came close to receiving financial settlements, I either talked myself out of it, thinking it was not worth the hassle, or someone else took it. Because I did not want to feel greedy, I did not fight harder in some instances when it might have changed the outcome if I had.

One of the original attorneys who handled the fraud case called to congratulate me that it had been won. I told him I did not end up with the money, and he was stunned. When my ex-husband called, he also thought the children and I were set for life. When I told him the outcome, he said he just could not believe it.

In the settlement of the school's lawsuit, I received a very small amount of money—vastly different from what I had anticipated when I began. Once again, I had to train my thoughts on the Lord and all that exalts Him, not what tears away at my heart. If I had let that disappointment linger, who knows what evil things it would have sown? I know, beyond any doubt, that my God will always take care of me.

MINISTRY AGAIN?

GOD OFTEN SENDS US BACK TO PLACES OR SITUATIONS IN ORDER TO TEACH US something or to heal us. This is a far cry from falling back into something negative. Moses ran from Egypt as a young man. When he went back, it was to deliver his people. Jonah ran from his missionary work in Ninevah, but when he went back, he saw God bring salvation to the nation.

I had to go back to people again, and so do you. That is what God took care of at the mall. As I worked there, I wondered if that business would really take off. During the summer months of 1998, as the gift market fell flat, a friend must have grown concerned. She told another friend, who told her friend, and pretty soon someone at the Christian Men's Network was in casual conversation with a friend who said, "Marte Tilton needs a job." When I received the call from the person who was then leading Christian Men's Network, I said immediately, "You don't want me." Although my heart had never left the ministry, I simply could not imagine working in a ministry again, much less being wanted by one.

I met with various board members, all of whom tried to convince me that Dr. Cole needed me and wanted me to work for him. Every time I repeated, "You don't really want me." Finally Dr. Cole met with me, and I got to say it to him, "You don't want me." But all of them persisted. Thrown into a quandary, I spent weeks praying and wondering what to do. I had hired help at the cart that I knew I could depend on to keep that business going. Many other concerns cropped up.

I warned Dr. Cole that it was very possible my name would be spread all over the newspapers in a short time because of the school lawsuit. I did not want it to taint the ministry he had built over the years, which has an unsullied reputation for integrity and Christlike living. He said he did not care; just come and help. I warned him that I still had lawsuits to work on and could not put in a full week's work. But he said he did not care; just come and help.

After working at the mall for less than a year, I found myself with great trepidation putting on a business suit and driving my dirty car down to the Christian Men's Network to start work talking to ministry partners and managing people once again.

God uses trials and crises to hold a mirror to us so we can see what is really in our hearts. When we submit to Him during these times, He is able to correct our characters and direct our paths. Dr. Cole says, "The quality of the product depends on the quality of the material used." What materials, what abilities, what gifts are in our lives with which we can glorify God?

It is true that legal matters have pursued me. There is always another paper to sign or another attack to repel. It has been nine long years, and I am still getting phone calls from lawyers about settlements and suits. But it is also true that since my days at the mall, I have never gone a week without people telling me they love me, are praying for me or care in some way about me. Why would I concentrate on the losses when God has given me such a wonderful blessing—being loved by others again?

I did not end up with what I could have had or perhaps what I should have had. But I have ended up with what I have needed because Christ has provided it for me. I walked away from that school lawsuit without a lot. But I left with a tremendous blessing. I released the money in the spirit realm, planting it as a seed, and I know it will come up again in my life. I forgave everyone involved, even if they had done nothing wrong, just to clear my spirit, and I asked God for His mercy and His help. He promised to give me all the things I need. Money runs out. God's blessings never do.

I keep applying the principles of God. I keep tithing and

sowing with what I have, doing what I can each day. God has sustained me. If I continue following His commandments, giving to Him and to the fatherless and widows, He will give back to me. He will promote me. He will protect me. Being obedient to His Word allows me to lay claim to His promises.

Every Sunday my pastor tells us to hold up our Bibles and declare that the Word sets us free; we are givers and not takers; we are the head and not the tail; we are above and not beneath; we will be blessed of God. I guess I have a little streak of rebel in me after all, because I change the last part to, "I *AM* blessed of God." *Because I am!* In the now, today, I am blessed.

You can say the same for yourself. Be grateful for every "little" blessing you have. Do what you can each day. Trust God to take care of the rest.

CHAPTER 12

LEARNING
TO WALK IN LOVE

ERPETRATORS ALWAYS MAKE VICTIMS FEEL THAT IT IS THEIR FAULT OR THEIR problem. Satan is a perpetrator, an abuser. He always comes to accuse us. When we fall, he blames us for falling. He whispers in our ear, "It was all your fault. See, you weren't such a good Christian after all." I was surprised by these tactics, but I should not have been. They are the reason the devil is the devil. And I was surprised by people who would knowingly lie, seek to victimize others and sin against God. But again, I should not have been.

It is Satan who commits *fraud* against us, meaning a deliberate deception perpetrated for unlawful or unfair gain. We become victims by being subjected to fraud. We become bilked, gulled, duped and gypped by the ultimate swindler, Satan. I became an easy victim through misplaced trust and by losing sight of whom I was created to be. God has a way of escape for us. Maybe you have wondered, as all victims do, "Why me?"

Many believe we will go through life trouble-free once we are saved, because Jesus fought the devil and won. Or we may believe we are exempt from troubles because we give, pray or are faithful in teaching. When the crisis comes, what a rude awakening! Suddenly we are no longer the *victor,* but the *victim.*

If we have never faced trials ourselves, when others go through them, we may excuse them away, saying there was a reason for theirs, but it would not happen to us. Jesus said, "In the world ye shall have tribulation: but be of good cheer; I have overcome the world" (John 16:33). Yet we tend to condemn others based on the little we know or see. We may even believe the news media on such occasions, which we hardly believe the rest of the time.

We can probably reach a million conclusions about any situation, and not one of them would be God's. One of the worst is, "They didn't have enough faith." Even Kathryn Kuhlman, the great healing evangelist, said that to suggest someone was not healed for lack of faith was the cruelest statement we could make. We simply do not know what is happening with others from God's perspective, nor is He obligated to tell us.

The Bible tells us that God "makes His sun rise on the wicked and on the good, and makes the rain fall upon the upright and the wrongdoers [alike]" (Matt 5:45, AMP). Storms will arise. People will persecute. But why? What is His purpose for trials? Unsuitable answers abound. Friends inevitably try to help with, "God is trying to teach you something." Or, "You're going through it so you can teach others." Or, "Don't ask why."

The only definitive reason I have found for trials is to test our faith. I certainly never expected to have a trial that tested my faith to this degree, because I thought I had so *much* faith. The apostle Peter said:

> Blessed be the God and Father of our Lord Jesus Christ, which according to his abundant mercy hath begotten us again unto a living hope . . . to an inheritance incorruptible, and undefiled, and that fadeth not away, reserved in

heaven for you. . . . Wherein ye greatly rejoice, though now for a season, if need be, ye are in heaviness through manifold temptations: That the trial of your faith, being much more precious than gold that perisheth, though it be tried with fire, might be found unto praise and honour, and glory at the appearing of Jesus Christ.

—1 Peter 1:3–4, 6–7

We must accept responsibility for ourselves, but we must avoid the role of the victim. Victims accept the blame for the trials instead of seeing them through God's eyes. Trials test and purify our faith and character, ensuring we are strong and pure. Fire purifies gold. Our faith is far more precious to God than gold.

The Victim

Late in 1993, as the sixty-day probationary period of my divorce came to an end, I took that trip went to Florida to clean out our vacation house. Some people came to help, and we sorted through everything, carefully leaving Bob whatever he would need, because he intended to live there until the house sold. I locked up the house, then sat in the 1989 Mercedes, which I still drive today.

The hot sun baked through the black roof of the car, making me feel a little wilted on the outside—almost as wilted as I felt within from the emotions of separating twenty-five years of marriage into stacks of "his" and "mine." I had steeled myself against the emotions for months, but now I felt the full force of them, along with the loneliness, the uncertainty and the sudden sadness brought on from a deep revelation that I was witnessing a death.

My cell phone rang, jarring me back to the new reality of my world, and I instantly recognized the voice of one of the lawyers. Her words cut into me like a knife. "So, Mrs. Tilton, how does it feel to be a single white female?"

To the lawyers I worked with, it seemed their attitude was "the one who ends up with the most money *wins*." People thought our divorce was a strategic legal maneuver. They were always looking for what we were up to, for the angle we were playing. From what I could tell, it never occurred to them that what I was up to was raising my children single-handedly and trying to do the right thing, regardless of what came my way.

The first time I felt like a victim—and a complete fool—was three months after my divorce when I received the first of a new kind of lawyer's calls. The lawyer said, "You're on your own."With just one call, the side agreement to the divorce was reneged, and my salary vanished. After that, pretty much monthly, calls came from the office of the church's lawyer telling me of another benefit that was being stripped away from the school—no more janitorial services...no more watering the football field. All the promises, assurances and vows I had received before signing and agreeing to slip away quietly disappeared overnight.

Besides the financial onslaught, wave after wave of personal attacks came. Whatever I did, wherever I went, whomever I spoke to, it seemed the church's lawyers would call. "Why did you go to that church?""What were you talking to So-and-so about?""If you do such-and-such again, we're going to have to do this-and-that." So many calls, so many threats, so many violations of my person, it has since congealed into a filmy memory.

Apart from the lawyers, people around me repeatedly said, "Marte, you are so dumb." Many of the people I worked with and for told me that everything was my fault. My ex-husband was living on the beach in Florida, but I had stayed behind, so I faced all the fury people felt toward him.

Inwardly, I felt like a fool, and I was certainly treated like one. I had lived in a bubble, thinking everyone else was trying to do right. Until I found myself in the dark pit, I never realized that was where I was headed. Truly I was naive.

Yet these were people whom I had trusted. Some of them had worked side by side with me through many late nights to ensure the church finances and administrative practices were in order. Some had fought side by side in the legal trenches, working diligently on the same team to ensure the church was not damaged. I thought we had a relationship like combat buddies who remain loyal to one another for years after the war. Just because one of the team wanted to divorce me, I did not know and could never have imagined that the rest would plot against me. These were my "friends"!

"I could have handled it had it been one of my enemies," King David said after being betrayed. "But he was my brother with whom I walked in the house of the Lord." (See Psalm 55:12–13.)

NO LONGER THE VICTIM

DURING OUR STRUGGLES, SO OFTEN WE HEAR *WHAT WE ARE NOT*. WE SEE what we lack. We feel what we have lost. But who are we? A victim accepts the blame. A victim receives the shame and degradation of others as something deserved. When that victim mentality starts to set in, it is time to ask God who we really are.

Realizing what is in our own character is both a tremendous opportunity and a struggle in any trial. It may come as a shock to discover that we are not the people we thought we were. God created us uniquely. He gave us our own gifts and talents. He knows the special personality He gave us—how we are wired. He knows if we are shy or bold, intellectual or emotional, neat or messy. He knows and cares about all those little things because He knows exactly how He created us in our mother's womb. He also knows everything that has happened to us since we left there! Nothing we discover in ourselves comes as a shock to God—only to us.

We will all find weak areas when we look honestly within ourselves. In those areas of weakness, Christ can become strong (2 Cor. 12:10). We can never be good enough, work hard enough or pray long enough to be strong enough. Never! We are completely dependent upon Jesus to live His life through ours and to fill in all our gaps.

When my husband and I started in ministry in 1974, I was shy and easily intimidated. I remember being so self-conscious that when John Osteen called me in front of the church right after we started, I wanted to dissolve into the floor. I never wanted to be noticed, much less be a star.

As I grew in Christ, when I read God's Word, I simply believed it. What God's Word told me to do, I did. What others told me I should do as a minister, I did. People would then say, "You're so strong and self-confident!" A sense of confidence developed, based partly on my faith in God, but also on the feelings I had about the good spiritual covering I was under. But as I listened to others, without the slightest awareness, I become more and more of a person created by those around me, either by role-modeling, teaching, intimidation or even through their silences.

I had made habits of eating the right foods, dressing, walking and talking in certain ways, managing business after a certain model and, of course, exercising every day, trying to please myself and others, not God. These externals created a tremendous sense of security. Some security! It so easily vanished. Just as John Osteen had said, Jesus had to become my security.

As I struggled through the lawsuits, divorce and rebuilding of a new life, everything that had worked for me before would work no more. My confidence in attorneys, my career, finances, my husband—even the United States justice system!—everything was stripped away. No wonder they call that feeling "having the rug pulled out from under you!" Only my confidence in God never wavered, but I certainly thought I no longer deserved His presence, and I did not feel His presence, either.

Even when I thought I was making decisions, I was not really calling any shots. I was easily manipulated. People would condition me ahead of time, anticipate my reactions, lay the trap, dig the ditch, set the bait and then watch me fall—which I did with pitiful ease. Recognizing this was as hard a blow as the external insults. This is the worst—when you are no longer comfortable even alone at home, peering out from under your blankets, watching "Lucy" reruns!

After all I had worked to create in myself, when I came under the intense pressure of circumstances, I made many wrong decisions. The relationship I thought I had with God was not complete. The person I thought I was did not exist. After all my faith, my devotion, my service and my consecration, I discovered that the person I had become was not the person God had made.

WHOSE ARE YOU?

AS CHILDREN, WE VIEW OURSELVES ONE WAY, MOSTLY AS A REFLECTION OF OUR parents. When we marry, we see ourselves in another way, often directly related to what our partner thinks about us. When we enter various careers or schools, we see ourselves differently again, often adapting to become part of that climate or community. If we divorce, we see ourselves still another way. If we have been sexually, physically or mentally abused, our mind-set and self-image can go in a completely different direction.

All these life situations affect our perception of who we really are. The only solution is to come into right relationship with God and, through the Word of God, discover who we really are. Yet instead of examining ourselves, when change is imminent, we tend to look at other people and try to copy them. Or we look at our own circumstances and are too afraid to try what our heart tells us we can do. Or we reject the voice in our hearts and read reports about the job market, then launch into the computer industry when we really wanted to be a musician, a heart surgeon or a baseball player.

We are still God's child even if we have lost our position, health, spouse, family, friends, income, business, job, reputation, inheritance or name. We cannot escape Him. Who can remain a victim with such a marvelous heritage? Victims accept condemnation, think they always attract problems, feel life is unfair to them alone and refuse to allow Jesus to be the victor. Victims say things like, "If anything can go wrong, it will go wrong for me." Victims accept every problem as something they deserved or created, which closes the door to miracles and repels the supernatural. But the victim mentality can only take root if we lose sight of who we are— or whose we are.

In times of trouble, it is easy to lose your sense of spiritual balance, feeling that God might be at the bottom of your trouble. We must determine in our hearts that God is not our problem. He loves us, cares for us and will be with us in trouble. We must believe that He will never leave us nor forsake us.

> Why is my pain perpetual, and my wound incurable, refusing to be healed? Will you indeed be to me as a deceitful brook, like waters that fail and are uncertain? Therefore thus says the Lord [to Jeremiah], If you return [give up this mistaken tone of distrust and despair], then I will give you again a settled place of quiet and safety, and you shall be My minister; and if you separate the precious from the vile [cleansing your own heart from unworthy suspicions concerning God's faithfulness],

181

you shall be as My mouthpiece. [But do not yield to them.] Let them return to you—not you to the people.

—JEREMIAH 15:18–19, AMP

I heard Charles Stanley tell a story about packing up to go home after a photo outing. When he packed up and got to his car, he realized his car was locked with the keys in it. Glancing across the parking lot he saw a sign that said, "High Crime Area." Instead of giving in to the victim mind-set, he started saying, "Lord, You're in charge of my life. Lord, You're in charge of my life." He had already tried all the doors to the car, but as he prayed, he tried the doors again. The back door opened! He got his keys and safely got away.

Victims forget to say, "Lord, You're in charge." God does not automatically take every problem away. We have to ask Him to be involved in the problem and to deal with it. Inviting God into our lives, and recognizing His presence there, is not a one-time deal.

We have been bought with the blood of Jesus Christ (1 Cor. 7:23). We are precious to God. God purchased us at such a high price; He does not want us to be enslaved or victimized by the world or the devil. He wants us to live free!

You are not your own…For you were bought at a price.

—1 CORINTHIANS 6:19–20, NKJV

Abide in Me, and I in you.

—JOHN 15:4, NKJV

The Father will love them too, and we will come to them and live with them.

—JOHN 14:23, TLB

WE CAN LIVE FREE!

WHEN JESUS CAME AS THE PERFECT SACRIFICE TO PAY FOR OUR SIN AND resulting death, He made a way for us to overcome anything. All our sin, shame, temptations and trials were laid on Him. All the suffering of penalty He endured in His humanity. Toward the end, He asked in His flesh for that cup to be passed from Him. Then He said, "Nevertheless, not My will but Thine be done." (See Mark 14:36.) For whom? For Himself? No, for us!

Jesus bought for us our victory over any villain. Any villain that operates in this earth is always under the influence of Satan, the deceiver, accuser, manipulator and liar. Jesus stripped him of all power to harm us, so we do not have to be his victims. No matter what Satan tries to do to you, you do not have to be the victim.

Jesus also took our temptations upon Himself—the temptations to run, to escape, to move to another part of the country, to change our name, to sin, to blame others, to resent God, to wallow in self-pity and to believe that everything was our fault. He took care of everything that could ever come against us. The enemy always plays on our imperfections. He reminds us that we are not what God or man expects us to be—our character is not good enough, our body is not good enough, our mind is not good enough. But Jesus *anticipated* those imperfections and took care of them in advance!

One big thrill I had when pastoring was to spot people from our church in a restaurant and pay their bill. Can you imagine how great it must be to ask the waiter for your bill, only to hear, "That's been taken care of!"? That is exactly what Jesus has done for us. No matter what we ordered or what we ate— no matter how dark the night or how badly we have messed things up—we can go to God, and He will always tell us, "That's been taken care of."

It has not been easy to go through trials, far from it. Yet walking through them, I have become more aware of how He equipped me even while I was yet in my mother's womb. As I was being formed there, He created in me the ability to face each day of my life—and each trial I would face.

The apostle Peter suffered more than most of us ever will. He wrote, "His divine power hath given unto us...exceeding great and precious promises: that by these ye might be partakers of the divine nature, having escaped the corruption that is in the world through lust" (2 Pet. 1:3–4).

We can *live free* from the rottenness of this world—not be *victimized* by it! Peter says that to live free, we should add diligence to our salvation, then virtue, knowledge, brotherly love, and Christian love (v. 5). As these qualities grow, Peter promises that they will keep us from being unfruitful in this life and, in the end, will ensure the inheritance of our loving Savior. When we believe this, trusting God, then we can go to Him with anything...anything!...and He will take care of it.

CUTTING OFF THE ACCUSER

THE PERPETRATOR ALWAYS TRIES TO BLAME THE VICTIM. LIKE THE CHILD ABUSER or molester who says, "Don't tell anybody, because if you do I'll tell them it was you," or "You did something wrong, too," or "You will get in trouble," Satan will always come at us with "You did this wrong." "You're not worthy of God, your family, career, respect..." "You've done it now." "Everything is going wrong." (Everything may not be going wrong, but we are blinded to anything that is going right.)

When he is having a heyday, as he did with me, Satan throws in these comments: "Few are chosen, and you're not one of the chosen of God." "You aren't a minister. Why did you call yourself a minister? You don't deserve to be a minister." "You'll never change, but you need to change." (Generally followed by silence as we sit wondering what part of us needs to change.)

And for all of us, he includes, "God did this to you." Satan accuses God as much as he accuses us. As if it were God who raped, killed and destroyed.

Being human, we tend to meditate on what Satan says to us more than we meditate on what Jesus did for us. I had to learn to accept the conviction of the Holy Spirit for the sins I had committed, and then throw away the condemnation of the enemy.

The Word of God will repel any onslaught. You can believe God's Word. You can believe Jesus came to take all your sin and all your shame to the cross with Him. We must fight the victim mind-set and become identified with the righteousness of our Lord Jesus Christ!

THE DARK TUNNEL—DON'T GO IN THERE

GOD BRINGS US TO A POINT TO MAKE A CHOICE. IF WE WILL MAKE THE CHOICE, God will make a way.

During those early years after my divorce, I met some people who had lost their energy to fight. I compared myself to them and thought, *Well, if God hasn't helped them after all this time, who am I to think I can get out of this?* Some were far more talented than I, yet had never succeeded in life since a failure occurred.

We were all cynical together. We would sit around and talk about comments some preacher made. We would say, "He hasn't been where I've been, so he doesn't know anything." That kind of talk, that reasoning, that cynicism kept me in the tunnel. Living there was the worst thing anyone could ever experience, and that was no one's fault but my own. No one forced me into that place. Those thoughts and spoken words may have opened the door—wide—but I willingly walked through it.

I finally started to pull back. I was sick of people saying, "God won't do anything for you," or "It's your fault." And I was determined to get out of this darkness. I realized I needed to make the break, get on my own and find the way out of that tunnel.

In December 1996 I had said aloud, "Lord, I don't know how I'm getting out of this tunnel, but I'm getting out!" Then I realized as long as I was at the school, other people would be in control of my every move.

After striking an agreement with the school board in July 1997, I resigned, not knowing exactly where I would go. They asked me to help transition the new headmaster, but that was the nastiest professional experience of my life. Two weeks later, I left the school completely, taking my children to safety elsewhere. That's when I ended up in the mall with the bunnies.

About the same time, I decided to attend Kenneth Copeland's Believers' Convention. On the second morning of the conference, as I drove around the bend of Highway 121 toward the Fort Worth Convention Center, suddenly I felt something close behind me with a giant spiritual "WHOOSH!" Miraculously, a spiritual breakthrough occurred, and I was once again in the light!

No matter how far you have gone, or how long you have lived in that dark tunnel, God's light is all around you. Be diligent to fellowship with God, day after day, even though you may see no differences in your circumstances. His Word says darkness and light are just alike to Him because He is the Light (Ps. 139:12). The Holy Spirit will show you a way out, and God will plant your feet upon the rock of righteousness that Jesus purchased for you—if you will allow Him.

HEALED

I DID NOT KNOW HOW TRULY "HEALED" OR "DELIVERED" I WAS UNTIL I HAD AN interesting personal experience. After my body endured so much stress, I needed surgery, which resulted in weight gain. For months I refused to buy any new clothes. I kept exercising every day as I always had, and I did not change my eating habits. But I could not get back into my clothes. Suddenly, one dress size larger, I looked like a different person to myself. I had

had a nice wardrobe for television and events, and those clothes hung in my closet condemning me, telling me daily that I was no good.

Finally one day I cried out to God, "What am I going to do to get back into these clothes?"

God spoke softly to my spirit, saying, "Those clothes represent what you became, not whom I created you to be."

Suddenly I realized I was accepted as I was, for who I was, regardless of what size I was. I did not have enough money to buy a new wardrobe, but the clothes were mostly designer wear, and I got the bright idea to sell them. With new clothes and a new sense of who I am in Him, I am becoming more of the person God really created.

"I am" statements can give life, or they can be deadly. "I am fat." "I am depressed." "I am unlovable by others." "I am a failure." We encounter such things out in this world and embrace them as our "identity," which is a lie. Out of the heart, the mouth speaks.

Sometimes we need to stop everything and cut off every outside voice to take stock of who we really are. "I am the righteousness of God in Christ." "I am more than a conqueror." "I am being transported from glory to glory." "I am blessed of the Lord." "I am accepted in the Beloved."

Who we are is first discovered by whose we are. Then comes the marvelous journey to find all the good things He has planted in our hearts.

FIND GOOD FRIENDS

WHEN I LEFT THE CHURCH AND ITS ADMINISTRATION IN 1993, MY FRIENDS WHO stayed behind told me they were basically instructed to choose their loyalties. Friends who would not renounce me were fired. Others stayed as self-appointed "spies." Some were true intercessors who wanted to pray as they went down with the ship. And still others were false friends. I remember asking one former friend why she stayed and why she said bad things about me. She answered, "I have a house payment to make." Another acted like a friend, helping me sort through all my possessions and taking many of the nice things I discarded. Then she vanished.

I also witnessed the disloyalty of the media. As far back as when we lived in California in the late eighties, a few years before the 1991 *PrimeTime Live* telecast, we were already subject to media scrutiny.

Once, on a flight we took from Dallas to California, a man came to my husband's side on the plane and started up a conversation with him. We noticed, albeit too late, that the flight attendants had stopped going down the aisle where this man was. They were evidently tipped off or paid to leave this man alone. Across the aisle from us, a man had a laptop computer open, which we thought nothing of, but it turned out later to be fitted with a hidden camera. "Steve," the man "befriending" my husband while crouched in the aisle, was a reporter for *Inside Edition*.

As we stepped off the plane, to our surprise we were met with lights and media reporters. Steve then identified himself to us and asked for more of an interview. Quickly, the two people who had come to pick us up grabbed each of my husband's arms and ran through the crowd with him, outside to a waiting car. I was left behind.

I wandered over to the baggage claim, figuring I was on my own, when suddenly here came the lights and reporters after me. I left the building and started wandering in the parking lot, hoping to catch a glimpse of the car. The reporter followed me, yelling out questions. I saw no way out and finally wheeled around to face them.

"Steve," I said to the one who had introduced himself. "Why are you doing this? How can you even live with yourself?"

They immediately turned off the lights, and he started asking me to cooperate. After I repeatedly told him I had nothing to say, the car finally pulled up to pick me up.

However, for all the horrible experiences I had and the horrid way I saw people act, overall most of the Christians I knew were stalwart soldiers of the cross who pressed on in their own ways. My hat goes off to a single mother who refused to divide her loyalties or to leave the church under any circumstances. She had come to the church almost destitute, living hand-to-mouth while trying to raise her son. Her dream was to enroll him in the church school, Lexington Academy, and get him off to a good start.

As she applied the principles of God's Word that she learned through my ex-husband, like thousands of others she saw the circumstances of her life change. She learned she was an heir of God, and she set her sites higher than a menial existence. She soon commanded a very respectable salary at a reputable company. Eventually she enrolled her son in the school. It seemed as if every week this single mother would tell me of a new miracle in her life. She was like a walking "praise report." In my darkest hours, hers was a face I always longed to see, because just her presence reassured me that God would not leave me and that He was a good God.

She remained at the church as well as having her son in the school. She refused to renounce me, refused to leave her pastor and at the same time refused the new doctrines that were brought into the church. As a result, she was ordered to leave. But she would not leave! It was her church where she had raised her son, and she was going to stick like glue. I know she must have been a burr in the saddle of the new rank and file. I have nothing but admiration for the route she chose. She still calls to check up on me from time to time.

Choosing friends, and finding those whom we can really trust, is an acquired art that will help us through the crises of life. I have heard it said that if you have two really true friends in life, you are blessed. And, "Friends are a lot like dollars, easier made than kept."

For a pastor's wife, the best people to befriend are generally not those in the congregation. I learned early in ministry that I could not divulge personal things about myself to members of the congregation. Otherwise, when a church member does not want to do what the pastor wants to do, the same people who acted like friends will often take everything they know, blow it up and turn it into something else.

In developing true friendships, we have to accept people. Jesus accepts us as we are, but He does not leave us as we are. We accept people for who they are, but we allow Jesus to clean them up. And we become a listener. There is power in listening. Few friends will really listen to us. Those who will are true friends. They hear our words and read into them what we really mean. Then they offer counsel based on what they heard between the lines. True friends also keep confidences. They are not gossips. A true friend will honor a request not to tell anyone else.

True friends sharpen us with their feedback, challenges and encouragement. "As iron sharpens iron, so a man sharpens the countenance of his friend" (Prov. 27:17, NKJV). True friends practice forgiveness. The hatred, self-pity and resentment that develop from unforgiveness breed instability, but our friends' forgiveness lets us off the hook. (See Matthew 6:14–15.)

I had let myself become surrounded with ministry friends, lawyers who had become friends, staff friends—and little else. The lawyers betrayed me. Because the staff friends were forced to take sides, it became hazardous for me to reveal myself to them. My ministry friends largely ignored me, perhaps for lack of knowing what to say.

My family had stuck by me throughout the ordeal. When the *PrimeTime Live* report first aired, I knew my mother was dismayed, but she was a quiet woman and never said much. I was glad my dad was living while the church was growing and thriving and never saw what came of us. When the divorce came, I saw in my mother's eyes the devastation she experienced. I had nothing but my love for her with which to soften the blow. When her health deteriorated, my sister gave up her career as an executive secretary to move to East Texas and care for my mother. My other sister was around during those years, and although she was active in her life and family, as were my brother and his family, I know their prayers were with me. My mother died in 1996 while I was still in that dark tunnel and surrounded by lawsuits. Having my family around helped me through the grief.

My sister moved back to Dallas following my mother's death and helped me at the school, since I could not afford a secretary. She decided she did not want to pursue another career because she found helping her sister fulfilling enough. My daughter also came to work at the school after she was fired from her position at the church. The fact that I had family members working for me became a huge issue later in depositions. It was as if the lawyers wanted to cut me off from any help whatsoever.

By that time, God had shown me I had friends I did not even know I had. When I had nothing to offer them, they were there for me, just to befriend me and love me and see me through. One was Ava, who had once attended our church and moved out of town. When she had heard about the divorce on the news, she tracked me down and called just to say, "I'm here for you." Then she just would not let go. She called repeatedly, until a pattern developed. Today, we still talk on the telephone once or twice daily.

Another friend, Lynda, was a former church member who had just returned to the church. She had marched in front of courthouses on picket lines in behalf of the church. When she heard about the divorce, she tried to call my ex-husband, but he would not talk to her. So she called me, and we became fast friends.

Another Linda went with me almost every time I went to court. At one two-week trial, my husband and the church's attorney had not even come to court that day to hear the jury's verdict. The insurance attorney and I sat alone at the defendant's table, waiting to hear the verdict. I looked around the courtroom watching reporters. I asked the attorney why Bob and the church's attorney weren't there. It had never occurred to me that being there was a choice. The judge read the verdict—guilty on all counts! This was later overturned.

The insurance attorney said she would handle the press for me, which allowed me to escape through the back door of the courtroom. Linda and I raced down the street, then had a leisurely lunch, hoping the crowd would disperse. But when we returned, reporters and cameras were waiting in the parking lot next to my car. Once again, I was on my own, but God had provided a friend to see me through.

Don Clowers worked as the senior associate at the time my husband announced the divorce. Don had tried to mediate to stop the divorce and pleaded with my husband to go to counseling. Don told my husband that if he went through with the divorce, he would resign. True to his word, Don resigned the day the divorce was announced.

Another young couple named Ron and Annette always sent me birthday cards. Some years later, they were thinking about someone who qualified as a "spiritual mother," and they decided on me. They wanted to "honor their parents," meaning spiritual parents, so Ron started coming over to help me with odd jobs around my house that I could not do myself. They wanted to appreciate me, and I have nothing but appreciation and admiration for them. I still receive a beautiful note or telephone call every birthday and Mother's Day.

As I read the Word of God and talked with my friends about my crisis, I gained understanding. At first I could not understand how people could be Christians who preached against certain things, yet do every one of those things. With my friends I would scream and rant and carry on, "How could they do this?" Then I realized the subtle deception that had slowly occurred.

"Friends" You Do Not Need

All of Solomon's errors were based on his associations with people— his friendships, the gods he allowed his wives to serve, his conflicts and even his sexual appetites. The Bible tells us to have wise associations (Prov. 22:17; 24:6). Dr. Cole says, "Counselors determine the destiny of kings." Much of the compromise I experienced was simply in allowing others to do things my heart said was not OK. At one time, the counselors I allowed into my life were people who wanted what we had materially, not spiritually.

"Who has interfered with, hindered and stopped you from following the truth?" the apostle Paul wrote to the Galatians. "This evil persuasion is not from Him who called you." (See Galatians 3:1.) People who try to introduce their "gods" into our hearts have to go.

I have seen people start running with the wrong crowd out of sheer frustration. Sometimes it is easier to be accepted in the "party" crowd than in the church crowd. By the very definition of leadership, at some point leaders become one of the "few"— one of the minority. When that happens, sources for fellowship diminish. If they are not accepted in the way they want to be accepted, some leaders find it very frustrating, and may be tempted to align themselves with those with whom they are accepted. But there is never an excuse for giving our friendship to the ungodly simply because they seem to accept us. Those who agree with everything we do, no matter how good they look, are not good friends. Anyone who goes with the flow and does not speak up to tell us when we are about to fall off a cliff is part of the "wrong crowd."

We are not to make friends with people who are angry (Prov. 22:24–25). Angry people are all around us every day. We may make their acquaintance, but we are to go no further. I met many angry people when I found myself in the "dark tunnel" of despair. We are also not to associate with the perverse or with "whisperers." Perverse people sow strife, and whisperers separate friends. (See Proverbs 16:28.)

One difference between Solomon and born-again Christians today is that Jesus has come—we have a means to become intimate friends with Jesus. Jesus called us friends. He has made known to us everything He learned from the Father so we can bear lasting fruit (John 15:13–17). Jesus commanded us to love one another. This is one way to become friends with God.

FRIENDSHIP WITH THOSE IN CRISIS

IN THE INTENSE DAYS AND MONTHS FOLLOWING OUR DIVORCE, AS THE CHURCH WAS being shaken by false winds of doctrine, I heard about a steady stream of our old ministry friends who went to my ex-husband as I sat across the street in the school. It was very hurtful, especially as I was trying to deal with my children who were very hurt as well. I choose to believe they thought I was fine, taken care of and building a new life that did not need their support.

There were, however, several people who reached out to pray for me and my children. For those I am forever grateful. They have prayed for us, loved and encouraged us. Kenneth Copeland's daughter called one day and let me know they had been praying for me. She invited me to their yearly minister's conference. There Brother Copeland spoke a word into my life that I have meditated on and been encouraged by.

John Osteen called on several occasions, and would say, "Marte, this is your pastor. I just wanted to encourage you today!"

What do you say when you do not know what has happened? I know now. When we know someone is in trauma of any kind, we just drop them a note if we do not know them well, or pick up a telephone if we do.

I have had many, many people walk up to me whom I have never seen and say, "I am praying for you." Those are the most comforting, encouraging words a person can hear. Some have even told me they are praying for one of my children specifically. That touches me even more deeply.

We need to pray for people. Make contact with them. Do not avoid them. We can simply say, "What can I do to help?" Most of the time they will answer, "I don't know," or "Just pray for me." If they do not ask for specific help, we can make contact with them again to let them know we are still praying for them. As we do, the Holy Spirit will tell us if He can use us specifically.

I have a friend who divorced recently. I never know what kind of condition she is in, because I am not one of her closest friends, but the Lord sometimes gives me specific things to do for her. Whenever it happens, it always comes as a direct answer to one of her prayers.

GOD WILL SEE US THROUGH

AS WE CLEAR THE CLUTTER FROM OUR LIVES, PHYSICALLY, EMOTIONALLY AND EVEN relationally, God can clarify for us where He is taking us and what we need to do to get there.

I have a scripture marked in one of my Bibles, dated the month before my husband divorced me. It reads:

> You whom I [the Lord] have taken from the ends of the earth...You are My servant...[even though you are exiled]....Do not look around you in terror and be dismayed...I will strengthen and harden you to difficulties....Behold, all they who are enraged and inflamed

195

against you ... they who strive against you shall be as nothing and shall perish.... For I the Lord your God hold your right hand.... Fear not; I will help you!... Behold, I will make you to be a new, sharp, threshing instrument which has teeth.... you shall glory in the Holy One of Israel.

—ISAIAH 41:9–16, AMP

EPILOGUE

LET GO
AND GO THROUGH

AMILIES OF BIRDS CHIRRUPED IN THICK OLIVE TREES AS MARY Magdalene rushed down the path to the garden tomb where her friend was buried. Dressed in a clean, simple robe, she had no fear of being recognized as the wild-eyed woman who once had seven demons cast from her. Early that morning, even in her haste she had held up a lamp to look in the mirror as she did every morning and smoothed her hair as she struggled not to say, "You're trash." A real Man, the first she had ever encountered, had taught her she was a valuable person, and her sins were now forgiven. For many months she had followed the Man who wanted nothing from her but gave her everything, teaching her and thousands of others how to have a life she had never imagined existed.

Now, racing down the path with the early morning dew dripping off the olive leaves onto her long auburn hair, Mary shivered and drew her plain linen robe closer around her shoulders. She did not find the morning too cool, but the memory of His bloody body hanging on a cross just a few days earlier was too vivid. So much was left unsaid, so much she wanted to tell Him, so much more she wanted to learn, but He was dead. She had thought it impossible to cry anymore, but she stumbled as her eyes brimmed over once again. Wiping away the tears, she saw her friends waiting for her in the wide dirt pathway where the orchards intersected. No one said a word, but fell in step together, strengthened by each other's presence, as they had been for two days while they sat outside the tomb, waiting for the Sabbath to end so they could anoint the body. Suddenly, through the trees they saw a large, gaping black hole where the large stone that sealed the tomb had been rolled away.

"NO!" Mary screamed, and she raced inside the tomb. Spinning around to grasp its emptiness, she threw herself onto the cold stone floor with sobs of anguish.

"Don't be frightened," an angel said. Mary was startled, and looked up to see two angels, whose presence illumined the dank cavern. "He is not here because He is risen. Remember how He told you He would die and rise again? Now go tell the disciples."

Mary lunged for the entrance, and three of her friends who had been cowering at the opening held out their hands to help her to her feet. They looked at each other with bewilderment, but Mary saw on their faces they had received the news with joy.

"Come," one of them said, tugging on Mary's hand. "We must tell Peter and John."

Coming back from Peter's house, John outran the rest and stopped at the entrance to the tomb. Peter rushed past him into the empty tomb to see for himself if what the women had said was true. Mary's friends were now joyously talking about all the prophecies they had heard Him say about rising from the dead. Overjoyed, the little group headed back to the house with Peter and John running ahead, but Mary Magdalene stayed behind.

Standing alone near the tomb's entrance, Mary thought of failure after failure she had experienced, of men who were not true and had abandoned and betrayed her, of all the false starts and sudden ends she had encountered, and she realized she did not dare believe this good news that her Redeemer was alive. She was a woman who had been tainted by her past, and she was unwilling to allow herself to be hurt again. Looking back inside the tomb, she saw two angels once again standing there.

"Why are you weeping?" an angel asked her.

"Because they have taken away my Lord and I don't know where they have laid Him," Mary cried with a rush of emotion. Waves of anguish welled up from her heart. She choked back sobs as she turned and wandered blindly toward the sounds of the birds in the tops of the trees that were welcoming the rising sun. A gardener approached her.

"Why are you weeping?" he said.

"Sir," Mary answered, wiping her hand across her eyes, "if you've put Him some place, please let me know." Again tears flowed with painful sobs, and she turned to cover her face. The gardener looked tenderly at her.

"Mary," He said.

Instantly Mary spun, and in a single movement, she threw herself at His feet to worship Him.

"Don't cling to me," He said, gently stepping out from the embrace of her arms. Just then Mary's friends, who had thought better of leaving Mary alone, came through the trees and threw themselves at Jesus' feet as well.

"Go tell My disciples I will see them in Galilee," He told them before He disappeared into the trees.

"LORD, WHERE ARE YOU?"

WHEN MARY WENT TO THE TOMB, A GRAVEYARD, LOOKING FOR JESUS, SHE WAS really saying, "Lord, where are You?" I have cried a million times, "Lord, where are You?" My pain overcame any ability to see God.

Mary looked for Jesus where she expected Him, but she

could not recognize Him where He was. In the midst of the pain of trauma, we yearn to go back to the comfortable place we once knew, and we tend to look for Jesus in the familiar way we used to know Him. Because Jesus does not come in the way we expect Him, we do not always recognize His presence in our situation.

Jesus called her name, "Mary." That is what we need. We must have a personal encounter with Jesus and hear Him call our names. Then we can worship Him fully as Mary worshiped Him. For months, then years, I felt the Lord nudge me to get on my knees during my morning devotions. I kept shrugging it off, thinking I was being "superspiritual." When I finally made the decision to get out of that dark tunnel, Jesus met me on my knees. Because the urge to kneel was new to me, I had not recognized His presence in it.

Jesus did not want Mary clinging to Him, and He does not want us clinging to the way we once knew Him. He wants us to be ready to recognize Him in the new way He appears to us. When Mary was looking for Jesus, she was actually looking for her past. Our past is dead, and we must let it go. Reaching back is like looking into a tomb in which we will find no life. If we hold ourselves in bondage to the past, as if that is the only way Jesus can operate in our lives, then we miss the new way in which Jesus wants to reveal Himself to us and through us. Jesus was no longer going to be with Mary in the physical realm, but His Holy Spirit would literally indwell her. Jesus says to us in essence, "Don't look for Me the way I operated in the past, because there's going to be a better way that I work in your life."

We have to let go of the way we have known God in the past in order to walk into a future with God. In Jeremiah, God says He has plans for us for hope and a future. We cannot have the future until we let go of the past.

Jesus then told the women to "go tell." We may have known Jesus in a church, in the way He operated through a specific minister or how He revealed Himself in our own families, but Jesus is not confined to the old ways to which we have grown accustomed. When He appears to us anew, He wants us to go tell others where to find Him and how to recognize Him.

Nothing Will Keep Jesus Away

Jesus yearns for us to call on Him so He can bring us out of our pain. He suffered our shame and agony when He went to the cross. He wants to see His completed work in our lives. Our first responsibility is to call on Him, then He will show us what to do.

Peter and John returned to the home where the disciples had created a makeshift headquarters for Christ's followers. Several dozen had gathered by the time Mary and the women returned with news of seeing Jesus. Still more came and huddled inside with doors and windows locked for fear of what the Jews might do. The city outside was in an uproar looking for the body of Jesus. Suddenly Jesus appeared to them through the walls of the house and showed them His nail-scarred hands and His side.

A little more than a week later, Thomas listened to their reports about seeing Jesus, but he did not believe them. Like Mary's first reaction, he felt this was too good to be true. Even though he trusted Mary, he believed her emotions must have taken over her senses when she thought she saw Him. Worried, fearful and having nothing to celebrate, Thomas sat apart from the others and just listened to their stories of Christ's resurrection.

"I'd have to see the nail scars in His hands to believe all that," Thomas said.

Suddenly, through the wall Jesus appeared again. Thomas jumped to his feet in fright as the others fell to their knees to worship the Lord. Jesus walked right over to Thomas and said, "Touch My hands and My side, Thomas, and believe." Thomas touched Him and fell to his knees as well, ashamed that he had not believed Christ's power even over death. "Blessed are those who believe without seeing, Thomas," Jesus said. Then He sat with them, called them all by name, calmed their fears and told them what to do next.

Walls cannot keep Jesus from you. Once you call on Him, no locked door to your life, no trouble, no hurt, no prison wall or shame can keep Him from coming to you. Call on Jesus today. Let go of the past. He will call you by name, and He will come through the walls of your life; He will appear and do something entirely new to bring you into the future He has for you.

Jesus, I cannot "fix" my life on my own. I admit the mistakes I've made and the sins I've committed. I accept responsibility for what I've done wrong. Please forgive me. I admit that I need You desperately and depend on You to hear my cry. Thank You for hearing me, for being here with me. I trust that even when I cannot see You, still You are making Your way through the walls of my life. I commit to read and listen to Your Word, obey Your instructions, let go of my past, forgive others and myself and follow You into my future. Amen.

It's OK

Many are the afflictions of the righteous: but the LORD delivereth him out of them all.

—PSALM 34:19

As people of God, eventually we have to believe the Word of God, meditate on it and trust God to deliver us from all our troubles. Armed with forgiveness for myself in my heart and the armor of God in my spirit, life is once again livable and even enjoyable.

For so long I believed the problems surrounding me were my fault, so I lived with the shame, fear and confusion of that condemnation. I never spoke out because I never thought I had a voice. Every time I tried to come out of my "closet," I was threatened. Today, there is not much left with which to threaten me! God used one of my sons to tell me I could "come out," that it was OK to talk.

My children and I still receive ridicule for our name. But we are moving beyond shame into the fullness of God's salvation. I now hear from God again, and every now and then it seems He leaves a scent in my house to remind me of Him, like the fragrance of flowers.

And, after all these years, the mechanics where I have taken my car for regular maintenance finally found the oil leak that kept that silly oil light on. After eleven years, I am driving a car without an oil light on!

At least once a week I run across someone who knows me from the church years. They always say two things: It is nice to see me, and they still pray for my ex-husband. Even though he has been judged severely by the media, and probably by many people, Christians have acted with the mercy of God, forgiven him and prayed for him.

The Only Way Out Is Through

Shortly after the *PrimeTime Live* television program, I was shopping for a Christmas gift for my husband and came across a little Limoges paperweight with the inscription, "The best way out is always through." In my mind, I thought it said, "The only way out is through." My husband did not want personal belongings, so the little box became a personal promise to myself that I really could make it through. No matter how far I fell or how dark the night was that closed in on me, I believed it. I believe it for you as well.

> For I am persuaded beyond doubt (am sure) that neither
> death nor life, nor angels nor principalities, nor things

impending...will be able to separate us from the love of God which is in Christ Jesus our Lord.

—ROMANS 8:38–39, AMP

Nothing can deceive you, imprison you or defile you so greatly that you cannot have the land of your heart purified and become productive again. Nothing you have ever done, or had done against you, no embarrassment to your reputation, no accusations against you can diminish God's love for you. No pathway you have chosen, no pit you fell into, no foreign land you entered could ever take you out of the reach of a loving God.

Early in my Christian life—just a few days after the young people had come to our house and led Bob and me in the sinner's prayer—God assured me that He would never leave me nor forsake me. And He never has. Even though my path has not been easy, through each step I walked in the dark tunnel, God walked with me. Even when I could not feel His presence, He was there. And He will be with you every step of the path you are walking.

The memories will fade and the pain will subside as you bring all you have ever known or felt into the redeeming light of God's truth and life. You are greatly loved, your value has been set at an unalterably high price, and you are greatly sought after by our God. You can find your way back to Him and find your way through with Him. My prayer for you is that your life will become full of the fragrance of flowers.

You can experience more of *God's grace & love!*

If you would like free information on how you can know God more deeply and experience His grace, love and power more fully in your life, simply write or e-mail us. We'll be delighted to send you information that will be a blessing to you.

To check out other titles from **Creation House** that will impact your life, be sure to visit your local Christian bookstore, or call this toll-free number:

1-800-599-5750

For free information from Creation House:

CREATION HOUSE
600 Rinehart Rd.
Lake Mary, FL 32746
www.creationhouse.com

Your Walk With God Can Be Even Deeper...

With *Charisma* magazine, you'll be informed and inspired by the features and stories about what the Holy Spirit is doing in the lives of believers today.

Each issue:

- Brings you exclusive world-wide reports to rejoice over.
- Keeps you informed on the latest news from a Christian perspective.
- Includes miracle-filled testimonies to build your faith.
- Gives you access to relevant teaching and exhortation from the most respected Christian leaders of our day.

Call 1-800-829-3346 for 3 FREE trial issues

Offer #AOACHB

If you like what you see, then pay the invoice of $22.97 (**saving over 51% off the cover price**) and receive 9 more issues (12 in all). Otherwise, write "cancel" on the invoice, return it, and owe nothing.

Experience the Power of Spirit-Led Living

Charisma Offer #AOACHB
P.O. Box 420234
Palm Coast, Florida 32142-0234
www.charismamag.com